FULLERTON

a pictorial history

FULLERTON

a pictorial history

By Bob Ziebell

Title page: In this photo of the southeast corner of Spadra (Harbor) and Commonwealth—
probably taken near the turn of the century—the Stern and Goodman Store has expanded
operations, including construction of another store building to the south. Jacob Stern and Joseph
Goodman were now well on their way to establishing themselves as the foremost merchants of the
settlement era. Photo courtesy of Launer Local History Room, Fullerton Public Library

The Donning Company/Publishers
184 Business Park Drive, Suite 106
Virginia Beach, Virginia 23462

Richard A. Horwege, Editor
L. J. Wiley, Art Director, Designer
Elizabeth B. Bobbitt, Production Editor

Library of Congress Cataloging in Publication Data:

Ziebell, Bob, 1934–
Fullerton: a pictorial history / by Bob Ziebell.
p.   cm.
Includes index.
ISBN 0-089865-848-9 (alk. paper)
1. Fullerton (Calif.)—History—Pictorial works. I. Title.
F869.F94Z54   1993
979.4'96—dc20   93-39259
CIP
Printed in the United States of America

CONTENTS

For relaxation, Fullerton and area residents would spend weekends camping on the beach at "Anaheim Landing," which today is known as Seal Beach. As identified on original photo, the des Granges family of East Fullerton was no exception, being shown here at a campout in 1903. Photo courtesy of Launer Local History Room, Fullerton Public Library

FOREWORD

When the Board of Trustees of the Fullerton Museum Center contracted with the Donning Company to produce a history of the city of Fullerton, a few wags around town joked "what history?"

Those good-natured jests brought to mind an old friend, a true maple-syrup-in-her-veins New Englander, who scoffed at the notion that any part of Southern California had a "history." History, she would sniff, "is older than 100 years. It's Plymouth Rock, Valley Forge, Concord, and 'shots heard 'round the world.' "

True, no major battles for independence were fought on the landscape that now comprises Fullerton. No constitutional congresses met here to hammer and hone a document that would guide the growth and development of a nation. In fact, while these historic happenings were taking place some three thousand miles due east, very little in the way of activity could be found on the land that is now Fullerton, save for the passing of the occasional Gabrielino Indian, coyote, or perhaps a herd of cattle from a nearby rancho on its way to better pasture.

So, indeed, why a history of Fullerton? The answer is simple: What happened in Fullerton was a direct result of all that took place in my friend's beloved New England. The pioneering spirit which gave rise to a new nation was the same force that would see the founding of countless cities like Fullerton across the country. The settlers, those believers in Manifest Destiny who pushed west, bringing with them homes, schools, churches and businesses, fought hardships every bit as daunting as the Bunker Hill patriots who stood firm against an army of red-suited invaders. And the history those settlers made—the founding of Fullerton and the other Southern California communities which sprang up in the same period—is as essential to the telling of our national story as the chapter that begins with the landing of the Pilgrims off Massachusetts.

And, thus, this book. To write Fullerton's history, the museum trustees have selected an ideal candidate. Bob Ziebell, like the settlers he writes about, is a transplant to Fullerton, coming here from Minnesota in the 1950s. (In California terms, that's sufficiently long enough to be considered a "native.")

With more than twenty-five years to his credit as a reporter and editor on the local daily newspaper, Bob is well acquainted with Fullerton, its people, and the qualities that we who live here think make Fullerton a very special place to call "home." Using the skills honed as a newspaperman, Bob has been able to sift through reams of historical material and present a view of Fullerton that is interesting, entertaining, and eminently readable.

So, when you open this book to chapter one, fight the urge to camouflage the cover with the dust jacket of a tome about some seemingly more "legitimate" historical event. Fullerton's story—and that of all the small cities and towns across this country—is an integral part of the patchwork quilt that is America. It's a story that helps us understand who we are. And, more importantly, where we are going.

Sylvia Palmer Mudrick
Public Information Coordinator, City of Fullerton

PREFACE

This book was well under way when I ran across some pertinent words regarding the writing of history. Edwin H. Cates, Ph.D., in his book *A Centennial History of St. Cloud (Minn.) State College*, published by Dillon Press, Minneapolis, Minnesota, said: "The obligations of an historian are three-fold: (1) to answer questions about the past; (2) to create interest in the past on the part of the reader; and (3) to show how the present evolved from the past." While not claiming "historian" status, I have none-the-less tried to meet those "obligations" in assembling this book.

Fullerton, typically, is many things to many people—"home, sweet home," a business address, a job location, a college degree, or simply a stop on the railroad line. The *Orange County Register*, in its seventy-fifth anniversary publication, *LEGACY, The Orange County Story* (1980), said, "the real roots of Fullerton repose in the characters, odd or admirable, that followed the first surveyor's stake pounded into an open field, green and gold with wild mustard. . . ." Indeed, the people make the city—different people from varying backgrounds and many walks of life, with differing ideas and talents. They laid Fullerton's foundation, presided over its transformation from grazing lands, through agricultural and citrus center and major rail shipping point to a community of diversified commercial and industrial enterprise and quality residential development. The story of Fullerton is a story of its people.

And, people made this book possible. One could not tell Fullerton's story alone; it required help from many sources. Because that help was so amply forthcoming, any attempt at an individual listing would surely be incomplete. But I must thank the Fullerton Museum Center board, its director Joe Felz and staff for their support. My gratitude to Sylvia Palmer Mudrick for her confidence. And, I would certainly be remiss in not acknowledging the consideration and encouragement of the Fullerton Public Library staff, particularly the recognized expertise and highly valued advice of Evelyn Cadman, rightfully considered a "Fullerton treasure" by those studying the city's history.

Finally, as we are about to embark on Fullerton's historic journey, I would like to cite words written ninety years ago. On February 4, 1904, just after voters created the city, a *Fullerton Tribune* editorial expressed what some would say amounts to a credo, words which remain applicable today and provide a guideline for whatever follows:

"And we should all—every man and woman among us—stand together to make our city of Fullerton a splendid, sturdy, thriving, enterprising community, to which the tourist and settler alike will wish to come, in which capital and labor will find steady profitable investment and employment, and where hundreds of contented, happy homes will eloquently testify to the peace and good which shall prevail among us. . . ."

Facing page: George Amerige said in a story written in 1937 that it was he who "installed the first water system" on the Fullerton townsite, but many residents thereafter met their own needs. Shown is the private pump house and water tank at the William Starbuck residence. Photo courtesy of Launer Local History Room, Fullerton Public Library

—*Bob Ziebell*

Ferocious-looking—and acting—saber-toothed cats were among animals which, fifty thousand years ago, roamed the lands now comprising Fullerton. Fossil remains of the big cats, nearly as large as today's ponies, have been found in the area of Ralph B. Clark Regional Park and are on display at the park's Interpretive Center. Illustration by Gail Lee Ziebell

CHAPTER I

PRELUDE

The Setting

Snuggled against the foothills at the edge of a coastal plain, lying softly atop a deep alluvial surface of rich soil, are the lands comprising what modern maps tell us is the city of Fullerton, county of Orange, state of California, U.S.A.

But for most of the world's history, these lands rested under ocean waters guarded by huge sharks—not unlike the great whites of today—whales, dolphins, and other sea life. Hundreds of thousands of years later, the land that emerged from beneath the waves would produce some of the best walnut and citrus crops on the world market and the fossilized remains of the old marine life would gusher up from far below the earth's surface in a new form—we would call it oil.

It was, perhaps, seven hundred thousand years ago that the earth rose and the sea receded, leaving a great, grassy flood plain with lakes and ponds which played host to giant mammoths—larger than the elephants of today—and vicious saber-toothed cats, and to lions similar to the African lions of today as well as the mountain lions which still inhabit the area, and a rare breed of llama, and camels, very large bison, wolves, coyotes, ancient horses and antelope, weird-looking sloths and tapirs—and the opposums of forty thousand years ago which remain with us today.

When these animals roamed the plains and foothills—more than forty thousand and perhaps as long as four hundred thousand years ago—the terrain was different than we see today, with the mountain ranges to the north and east enveloping the foothills of today. Heavy, turbulent water runoffs, on a furious flight to the sea, would often trap these animals, burying their bodies under the mountain soil, where, uncovered today, their bones serve as evidence of their very existence.

Such evidence—marine life fossils, soil which could only have come from the distant mountain ranges, the bones and teeth of a wide variety of ancient land animals—has been found in Ralph B. Clark Park in the Coyote Hills at the Fullerton-Buena Park border. Volunteers catalogue and preserve the material at the Interpretive Center in the park where it is displayed for all to see. There is the upper arm bone and a portion of tusk from a massive mammoth—eleven feet tall at the shoulder—who lived here fifty thousand years ago; shark teeth from perhaps a million years ago; the jawbone of a species of llama found in only six places in the world: here, Florida, Texas, Bolivia, Ecuador, and Brazil; a tooth from a tapir, a type larger and older than those of the La Brea Tar Pits; the huge "toe" of a sloth who lived here fifty to sixty thousand years ago. And there are the tiny fossils of small sea urchins which tell so much about other life; and the bones of a condor, much larger than those of today—and, fascinatingly, much more.

But when the first humans arrived—a matter subject to speculation but perhaps as long as fifteen to twenty thousand years ago—they found these lands nurturing grasses, wild mustard and bushes, with some oak woodlands along streams on the plains areas and chaparral as well as gnarled, low-growing broadleaf evergreen plants in the hills.

This tells us of a life before what our pioneer predecessors saw—a fertile valley topped by gentle, rolling hills which dip again toward the basin known as the La Habra Valley. The Coyote Hills to the northwest and Puente Hills to the north and northeast, had drained their rich soil across this broad expanse, and a river—the Santa Ana—had often sent its flood waters meandering over the valley floor, depositing life-giving silt and creating the rich alluvium which was to serve these farmers and ranchers so well.

And the pioneers, many of whom came here for health reasons, enjoyed a comfortable, semi-arid climate with about three hundred clear, warm days per year. The warm summers were almost devoid of rain; fall and winter bringing most of the, sometimes intense, rainfall averaging fourteen to fifteen inches per year. Frost was infrequent, but the hot, dry northerly and northwesterly Santa Ana winds of fall and winter more common—but, back then, of course, smog was nonexistent. Annual mean temperature is about sixty-three degrees fahrenheit.

The lesson in all this, if there is one, would seem to be that the many changes which have occurred in the 200-plus years since written history of this area began—which we are about to review—are miniscule when considered in the greater perspective of the last one million years on life's landscape.

Proof that ocean waters once covered what is now Fullerton is found in the discovery of shark's teeth in the digs at Ralph B. Clark Regional Park in the northwest area of Fullerton, adjacent to Los Coyotes Country Club. Illustration by Gail Lee Ziebell

This fossilized part of a mammoth leg bone (left) and portion of a tusk (right) were found in digging at "Elephant Hill" at Ralph B. Clark Regional Park on Rosecrans Avenue at the western edge of Fullerton. Photograph by the author

This is a photo of the bones found in November 1939, when workers were excavating the site of Fullerton City Hall at the northeast corner of Highland and Commonwealth avenues. Photo courtesy of Launer Local History Room, Fullerton Public Library

CHAPTER II

The Early Dwellers

Historians have had a penchant to report that "little is known about the early Indian inhabitants," or that "not much has been recorded about the early inhabitants" of the Fullerton area—then proceed to tell you quite a bit about them, albeit with some conflicting comments regarding their personal characteristics.

There is evidence of human habitation in Orange County as long as seventeen thousand years ago, which is the carbon-dated age of the "Laguna Woman's" skull, so named after its discovery in Laguna Beach. She may have been an early descendant of the Eastern Europeans who migrated across the ice covering the Bering Straits, or perhaps she came from the south, across the intercontinental land bridge.

These "true natives" were supplanted many years later by the Indians who greeted the Spanish explorers more than two hundred years ago. These peoples—later known in this area as *Gabrielinos*—were on the Fullerton lands at least as long as a thousand years ago.

The Indians used a language of the Shoshonean linguistic group and belonged to a large tribal family identified as the Uto-Aztecan, linking them to such tribes as the Ute of Utah, the Comanche of the plains and the Aztec of Mexico. A sub-tribal designation was the *Tongva*, a name given to those residing in the area stretching from Tujunga in Los Angeles County to Aliso Creek in Orange County and as far east as San Bernardino in the county of the same name.

Local Indians were organized into "patrilocal" bands, a dozen or so families of related blood based upon paternal lines. Their villages—called *rancherías* by the Spaniards—usually consisted of less than one hundred inhabitants. Each basic family unit—which often included many besides the immediate family, such as grandparents, widowed aunts or a daughter-in-law—lived in a single residence, dome-shaped, thatched huts called *wickiups* by the natives and *jacales* by the Spaniards. Father Juan Crespí, a diarist in Gaspar de Portola's 1769 expedition through the area, described them as looking "like half an orange."

The *rancherías*—cohesive enough for easy internal problem solving and large enough to provide mutual support and self-defense—usually sat in the center of the clan's resource (food gathering) area. Several of these villages would form what

The scene is from an Indian village typical of that which may have been found in the Fullerton area and with a setting similar to that of Sunny Hills Site No. 1. The woman at left is depicted removing the hard shells from acorns, a staple of local Indians, while another woman is returning with more acorns gathered from the surrounding countryside. Illustration by Gail Lee Ziebell

one historian called "tribelets"—small tribes numbering in the hundreds as compared to Eastern and Plains tribes which numbered in the thousands.

Fullerton area Indians were short, but muscular; their skin color was lighter than many other California Indians. They had flat noses and both the men and women wore their straight, most often black, hair long. Governor Pedro Fages thought they were "good looking." Clothing? In the warm weather the men and children wore none at all; the women wore two-piece aprons made of willow bark, grass fibers, or other materials.

They, indeed, lived off the land. The men hunted and fished; deer, antelope, rabbit, squirrel, skunk and other small rodents, grasshoppers, insects, or, as Father Crespí noted in his diary, "indeed, anything else that ran, walked, crept, crawled or wriggled" as well as quail, dove, and other small birds were food for local Indians. Women gathered and served—in various stewed and blended concoctions—the small insects, larvae and lizards from the prairies and crayfish from the banks of creeks. But acorns were the staple food of the Indian diet. They were gathered from the live oaks of the foothills—from groves which sometimes became the objects of clan battles for possession—and then were ground on stone mortars, leached, and eventually served in the form of mush or soup.

In Fullerton proper there have been several discoveries of Indian skeletons. Two—one more than fifty years ago, the other much more recently—have been the most extensively documented. In each case remains were dated to about a thousand years ago.

On November 7, 1939, while excavating for the new City Hall (now the police building at the northeast corner of Commonwealth and Highland) workers were startled to uncover human skeletal remains. The remains—dubbed "Fullerton Man" by the *Fullerton Daily News-Tribune*—were those of an Indian and were at least a thousand years old, according to John W. Winterbourne, who was then the archaeologist in charge of a museum being developed at Fullerton College. The remains were given to the college for preservation—except for an arm bone, which, in 1941, was placed, along with other artifacts and documents, in the cornerstone of the building.

Then, on January 15, 1992, a construction worker uncovered a skeleton while digging under a sidewalk on Commonwealth Avenue near the municipal airport. Judy Suchey, forensic anthropologist from California State University, Fullerton, aided in recovering about 95 percent of the skeleton and said it was that of a woman about four feet ten inches tall who was at least eighteen years of age when she died. The remains, she said, were at least four hundred and perhaps a thousand years old. The old Indian's *Gabrielino* descendants later reburied the bones near where they had been found.

The lands now comprising Fullerton apparently played host to more than one Indian village. One historic account of Portola's 1769 expedition said the group encamped at an Indian village "just west of Fullerton Road (Harbor Boulevard) a short distance below Brea Dam." And, earlier in the same year as the City Hall skeleton discovery—in March and April—Fullerton College and Fullerton High School jointly participated in a Works Progress Administration (WPA)–supported archaeological excavation of an Indian village site just north and west of the present Bastanchury Road–Malvern Avenue intersection, known as Sunny Hills Ranch Site No. 1. A short time before the excavation began, a Bastanchury Water Company employee had taken soil from the site for use at the Water Plant garden and had removed three skeletons. Excavators said a "most interesting" iron point or lance head, possibly of Spanish origin, along with a few flaked points, were found at the burial site.

This example of bedrock mortars from Orange County is located on the quad at California State University, Fullerton. A plaque provided by the Museum of Anthropology explains: "These grinding holes (mortars) were made by Indians while preparing food. Acorns were pounded into meal by using oblong stones (pestles). Bedrock mortars were used in Orange County between approximately 200 B.C. and A.D. 1750." Pestles were discovered on the Sunny Hills Site No. 1 dig conducted in March and April of 1939 near the current intersection of Malvern Avenue and Bastanchury Road. Photo by the author

Debris and fill from the roadbed of a Union Pacific Railroad spur line (still there) had covered a major portion of the camp. Nonetheless, a report on the "dig"—written by Louis Plummer, superintendent of schools, and the same John Winterbourne mentioned in the City Hall find—said a considerable number of stonework artifacts were found, such as manos, metates, and pestles—mill and grinding tools used in the preparation of food. And there were stone-flake objects, such as a small knife and arrowheads found. Bone artifacts were more unusual, in fact the only complete object was an awl which had been formed, most likely, from the splintered fibula bone of a deer. There were also some fragments of tibia bone instruments.

Another camp, perhaps a large one, was located to the north and east of the Malvern-Bastanchury site, but the Sunny Hills Ranch Site No. 1 excavators said the land, then part of the Emery Land Company, was planted to a young lemon grove and "cannot be investigated."

The *Gabrielino* designation for Fullerton's Indians came after arrival of the Spanish explorers and establishment of the missions. Orange County Indians north of Aliso Creek and in the domain of Mission San Gabriel became *Gabrielinos*; those south of Aliso Creek, in the domain of Mission San Juan Capistrano, became *Juanenos*.

The mission padres recruited neophytes (converted male Indians) from the *rancherías* and then tried to teach them new skills such as leatherworking, masonry, spinning and weaving, carpentry, pottery making, and blacksmithing. It was a very slow process and some did not take to it at all, fleeing back into the hills where they gathered and often schemed against the missions, raiding their lands for cattle and horses.

But the white man brought more than agricultural, cattle raising, and building skills to the Indian. He also delivered disease, prostitution, and gambling. California historian Hubert Howe Bancroft said, "It was a scurvy trick for civilization to bring its pestilence and foul disease to scatter among these simple savages." And, indeed, epidemics—principally of measles and smallpox—and venereal disease took a heavy toll among *Gabrielinos* ill-equipped to resist these unfamiliar diseases. During the mission period the Indian death rate exceeded the birth rate.

Slowly, surely Gabrielinos, as a cultural force, faded from the scene.

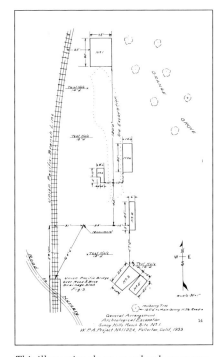

This illustration shows exactly where excavations were made on the Sunny Hills site. The Union Pacific Railroad tracks still exist, and so does the trestle over the Brea Creek Channel (lower left of drawing). Map from Report on Sunny Hills Site No. 1, *Launer Local History Room, Fullerton Public Library*

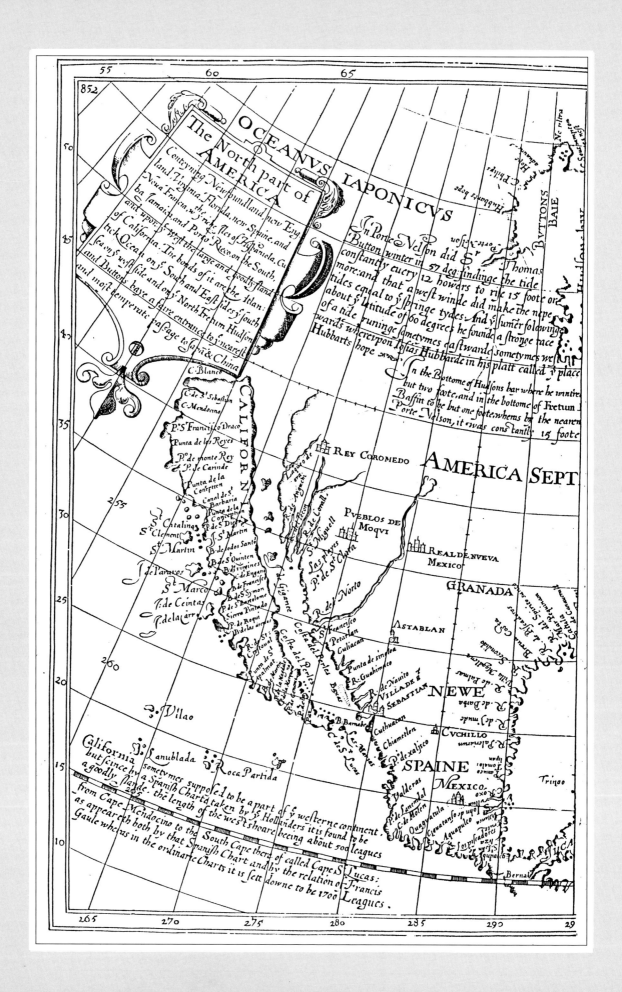

CHAPTER III

Exploration and Discovery

In a popular Spanish novel of the time—*Las Sergas de Esplandian*—author Garcí Rodriquez Ordóñez de Montaluo wrote, "Know, then, that, on the right hand of the Indies there is an island called California, very close to the side of the Terrestrial Paradise."

Those words, written circa 1510, must have leaped into the mind of Hernando Cortés, Spanish explorer and conqueror of Mexico, when, sailing along the west coast of Mexico in about 1535, he found what he thought was a large island standing boldly off the coast. He named it California and, although what he saw was not an island at all but rather the peninsula we know today as Baja California, the name stuck.

The name, then, was in place before discovery of what is now the state of California. Some histories hint that Spaniard Hernando de Alarcón, searching with Francisco de Coronado for the Seven Cities of Cibola, may have been the first explorer to set foot in the state—in 1540—but most often credited with the state's discovery is Juan Rodrígues Cabrillo, a Portuguese navigator in the employ of Spain, who sailed into San Diego Bay on September 28, 1542—just fifty years after Columbus arrived on the opposite coast.

The 1579 explorations of English navigator Sir Francis Drake along the northern California coast aroused Spanish concerns about land rights and they sent more explorers, including Sebastián Vizcaíno, who, in 1602, gave lasting names to San Diego, San Clemente Island, and Santa Catalina and traveled at least as far as Monterey Bay. He forwarded glowing reports of what he had seen and recommended colonization. The Spanish government later gave support to efforts by the Jesuit Order to establish a chain of missions in Lower California—Mexico—beginning in 1697.

The Jesuits were recalled in 1767 and the Franciscans took up the task. Father Junípero Serra, who had been serving as a missionary in Baja California and Mexico for eighteen years, was designated to lead the "Grey Friars" (named for the color of their religious habit). The diminutive (five foot two) Franciscan enthusiastically took on the job (an effort on behalf of the Crown as well as the pope) that would lead him to spend the rest of his life in California. In the

Facing page: Maps such as this one of "The North Part of America" which shows California as an island, probably reflected the influence on explorers of the early sixteenth-century Spanish novel Las Sergas de Esplandian. *Illustration from* Wilderness to Empire, a History of California, *by Robert Glass Cleland, published by Alfred A. Knopf, New York, 1944*

Father Junípero Serra was president of the California missions, established on behalf of the Spanish government by the Franciscan fathers. Father Serra headquartered at the mission in Carmel, but called the mission at San Juan Capistrano home from 1778 to 1783. The Serra Chapel, where the diminutive Franciscan with a crippled leg conducted mass, still stands and serves worshippers today. Father Serra died at the mission of San Carlos on August 28, 1784, about three months shy of his seventy-first birthday. Illustration by Gail Lee Ziebell

company of the leading Spanish government representative, Gaspar de Portolá, governor of Lower California, he would blaze the trail that opened the state to settlement.

The Spanish government was still concerned about the territorial threat posed by the English (and, increasingly, about Russian exploration in the north) and directed that Father Serra and Governor Portolá lead an expedition to Alta (Upper) California with the expressed purpose of establishing missions and *presidios* (military posts). The objective was to claim the land for Spain and convert the natives to the Spanish way of life, thereby creating loyalty to the Spanish Crown. This would lead to the first overland travels by white men in California—and right through the center of what is now Fullerton.

Four parties of Spaniards—two by sea, two by land—traveled from Lower California to rendezvous in San Diego. All encountered hardships and delays and the Portolá-Serra land party was the last to arrive, on July 1, 1769. On a hot afternoon thirteen days later—July 14, 1769—Portolá led a group of four officers and sixty-three men out of San Diego to establish an overland route to Monterey Bay. The party included two future governors of California— Lt. Pedro Fages (1782–91) and his successor, Capt. Fernando Rivera Y Moncado—and the grandfather of another (Juan Bautista Alvarado, grandfather of Juan B. Alvarado), as well as a Catalan volunteer by the name of José Antonio Yorba, destined to become the premier ranchero of Orange County.

Father Serra, nursing an ailing leg—the result of an infected mosquito bite, and an injury that plagued him the rest of his life—and facing responsibilities for caring of the ill and injured as well as establishing the mission at San Diego, was not in the party; he sent Father Juan Crespí and Father Francisco Gómez in his stead, charging them to locate potential mission sites and initiate contact with the Indian natives they hoped to convert and train. The diaries of Father Crespí and an engineer, Miquel Constansó, provide the first written descriptions of inland California, including the Fullerton area.

The group's travels through Orange County included events and created names that remain with us to this day. On July 22, 1769, the priests conducted the first Christian baptisms in California at an Indian village in what was named and to this day is called *Los Christianitos* ("Little Christians") Canyon; on July 24 one of the soldiers lost his weapon (called a *trabuco*) and another canyon was named; on July 26 the party marked the festival of St. Anne and named the valley before them in her honor. Then, on July 28, after experiencing a severe earthquake while encamped on a river bank, the name *El Rio del Dulcissimo de Jesus de Los Temblores* was given to the river. The name didn't stick, but the one used by the soldiers in honor of the valley, did—*El Rio de Santa Ana*—the Santa Ana River.

As the party continued on its route—later known as El Camino Real (usually interpreted as "The Kings Highway" but also as "The Real Road, The Royal Road" or "The True Road") and marked by the bell monument in the Harbor Boulevard median between Wilshire and Amerige avenues—they came to the Fullerton area on July 29. C. E. and Marilyn Parker report in *Orange County: From Indians to Industry* as follows: "Encamping just west of Fullerton Road (Harbor Boulevard) a short distance below Brea Dam, the expedition continued on July 30, in a northwesterly direction." (A commemorative marker at the mouth of Brea Canyon in Brea, about 4.5 miles north of the Brea Dam, cites that as the location of a July 31 encampment of the Portolá party.) What must it have been like, the Fullerton of more than two hundred years ago? Writer Doris Lee provided a vivid fictional image in a *Fullerton Daily News-Tribune* (July 19, 1969) story commemorating the two hundredth anniversary of the event:

Sgt. José Francisco Ortega reined in his horse at the base of the hill and his scouts pulled up beside him while they waited for the rest of the train to catch up.

The afternoon sun was high and the July air was still and soundless except for a slight rustling noise as the long column of men, horses and mules made its way across the grassy plain toward the waiting horsemen.

The grassy plain was Fullerton of 200 years ago. The hill was part of the string of rolling hills forming the north end of Fullerton and stretching west to Buena Park.

And the first white men ever to gaze upon this unblemished pastoral scene were now pushing through the grasses, led by one of Spain's best soldiers, Gaspar de Portolá.

As the padres thereafter continued with the establishment of missions, each a day's ride from the other, El Camino Real through Fullerton became a well-traveled route. One history reports the Franciscans scattered mustard seed along the trail in order to provide spice for the bland mission fare—and therein may rest the explanation for the tall mustard plants which so impressed the pioneers and covered the Harbor Boulevard—Commonwealth Avenue intersection where Edward Amerige, in 1887, drove the first survey stake for the townsite of Fullerton.

This mission bell, now located in the Harbor Boulevard median between Amerige and Wilshire avenues, marks the trail of "The Kings Highway," El Camino Real. The route between the missions was traveled by the padres in the second half of the eighteenth century and beyond, and became the major north-south route through Fullerton and much of Orange County for the early settlers. Photo by the author

The residence of Don Bernardo Yorba was a magnificent two-story adobe built in about 1835 near the old road through Santa Ana Canyon, north of the Santa Ana River, where it served as the hub of Rancho Cañon de Santa Ana and the social center of the entire area. This site housed everything from wine and cheese makers, to dressmakers, blacksmiths, carpenters, bakers, jewelers, plasterers, etc. From this headquarters, the innovative Don Bernardo introduced new methods of irrigation, established the first cemetery, watched over building of the first nonmission church and the first school off mission grounds in Orange County, according to LEGACY/The Orange County Story, *the seventy-fifth anniversary publication of the* Orange County Register. *Photo courtesy of Launer Local History Room, Fullerton Public Library*

CHAPTER IV

Missions and Ranchos

Mission San Diego de Alcalá (1769) was the first built and southernmost link in the chain and Mission San Francisco Solano de Sonoma (1823) was the last built and northernmost of twenty-one socio-economic centers stretching from San Diego to Sonoma, north of San Francisco Bay. They represented the first semblance of government in the emerging California claimed by the Spanish Crown.

Two other missions—La Purísima Concepción and San Pedro Y San Pablo—were built on the California side of the Colorado River at the Mexican border in 1780, but were destroyed in July 1781, during the historic Yuma Indian Massacre.

Soon a few—and, later, many—grants of grazing rights created the ranchos of book and movie lore and split the land further. The ranchos became hubs of activity in their own right, the centers for business and social activities for miles around. Together, the missions and ranchos brought order and discipline to life in California.

The missions were essentially a political creation. The Franciscan priests worked hand-in-glove with soldiers of the Spanish Crown to establish the outposts and convert the natives to the ways of Christianity—and Spain—primarily to affirm Spain's claims on the land, but also to head off Russian occupation from the north. Father Junípero Serra explained it clearly as he blessed the Bay of Monterey in 1770; the objective of the expedition, he said, was to "occupy and defend the land against the atrocities of the Russians." The lands were to be tilled into productive acreage; the Indians were to be converted and trained in the ways of the Spaniards—and then the new Indian citizens were to take over, converting the missions to *pueblos* ("towns") of the Spanish Crown. The latter, of course, never happened.

The two missions affecting Orange County were established within seven years after the Spaniards first set foot here. The first—on September 8, 1771—was Mission San Gabriel Arcángel, the fourth built and also the fourth link in the chain. Included in its jurisdiction were the lands of Fullerton, and with its founding began the land transformation process that continues to this day. The other was Mission San Juan Capistrano, on November 1, 1776, which controlled the lands extending south from Aliso Creek. (San Juan Capistrano, the seventh

The Mission San Gabriel Arcángel, opened in September of 1771, had jurisdictional control over the lands that later made up Fullerton. Mission San Gabriel, whose famous bell wall is depicted here, was one of the most wealthy of all the missions. Illustration by Gail Lee Ziebell

mission built and third in the chain, was actually founded a year earlier at a location about five miles from the present one, but was abandoned by order of the Spanish commander when word was received of a possible Indian uprising at San Diego and the troops were forced to return there.)

The missions simply took over; life revolved around them as they took control of the lands and introduced agriculture, cattle, sheep, and hog raising. The Indians were brought under the wing of the missions and taught skills needed to carry on their operation, including construction techniques, leathercraft, and candle and soap making. The finished products of these labors were traded to Yankee merchantmen for other foodstuffs, and clothing—and money—to enrich the mission.

The San Gabriel Mission prospered, becoming one of the most successful in terms of production and wealth. Long-horned cattle brought from Mexico were used to the fullest extent, i.e., meat for eating, hides and tallow for leather goods, candles, and soap. And there were the graineries, huge ones built on the grounds to store the wheat and grain. At its peak the value of Mission San Gabriel was placed at $110,000, an unusually high value for those days.

To the south, Mission San Juan Capistrano, home to Father Serra from 1778 to 1783, also flourished. The original church—"Serra Chapel"—still stands and is considered the oldest extant building in California; it is the only remaining church where Father Serra, president and founder of the missions, actually celebrated Mass.

The missions survived the transition from Spanish to Mexican rule in 1822 when Mexico proclaimed itself an independent republic, but later in that decade there began stirrings among Californians concerned about the economic domination of the missions. When the demand for return of mission lands to the public domain began to increase along with the number of migrating Americans, Mexico decided to take action. The result was the Secularization Act of 1833, a plan designed to return the lands to the now-converted Indians. But, it didn't work that way as the *Gabrielinos*, confused without the direction of their mission overseers, scattered. The Mexican government then pleaded with its citizens to take over the land by filing claims for grazing rights. The response was great and the Rancho Era was thrust full force upon Southern California.

The large ranchos granted as grazing lands—first by the Spanish and then by Mexican governors—eventually replaced the missions as centers for activity, but for some time they co-existed—usually, but not always, to everyone's pleasure. Only twenty to thirty such grants were made by Spanish governors during their tenure, but nearly eight hundred were made by Mexican governors. One vast Spanish grant of approximately three hundred thousand acres, which took in part of what was to become Orange County, was the one to Manuel Nieto by Governor Fages in 1784. Nieto heirs requested a division of these lands in 1834 and from them were created Ranchos Los Coyotes, Los Cerritos, Santa Gertrudes, Las Alamitos, and Las Bolsas. These names are recognizable to present-day residents in the form of cities and areas located to the west of Fullerton.

Another Spanish grant, covering lands to the southeast of what is now Fullerton, was made in 1810 to that Catalan soldier of the Portolá party, José Antonio Yorba, and his nephew, Juan Pablo Peralta. The 62,500-acre tract, known as Rancho *Santiago de Santa Ana*, was located south and east of its Santa Ana River boundary, stretching all the way to the ocean. The Yorbas built their home on the east side of the river where it bends to the south and the Peraltas located on the south side of the river adjacent to the area now known as Peralta Hills. Twenty-four years later—1834—Yorba's third son, Bernardo, was awarded a Mexican grant of 13,328 acres lying on the north side of the river, across from the Peralta portion of the 1810 grant. It was known as Rancho Cañon de Sana Ana.

Three years after that, in 1837, the Fullerton lands were included in a grant made by Governor Juan B. Alvarado to Juan Pacifico Ontiveros—the rancho known as *San Juan Cajon de Santa Ana*. Not only would Fullerton eventually spring from this rancho, but so would the cities of Anaheim, Placentia, and Brea.

Juan Pacifico Ontiveros was born in the pueblo of Los Angeles, which his grandfather, Josef Antonio Ontiveros, had come to California to help settle. Pacifico was a former soldier, following in the footsteps of his grandfather and father, Juan Patricio Ontiveros. It was the latter who first applied for a land grant in 1833, after completing his military obligation and seeing service as mayordomo ("overseer") of Mission San Juan Capistrano and as a supervisor on Rancho Santa Gertrudes. His request was protested by Juan José Nieto, son of Manuel who had been granted the rights to Rancho Los Coyotes. A subsequent battle over boundaries continued through numerous legal procedures and was still unsettled when Don Juan Patricio Ontiveros died, probably in late 1834 (the exact date was not recorded).

Pacifico, born in Los Angeles on September 24, 1795, served in the military for an extended period. He married María Martina Osuña of Santa Barbara on November 24, 1825, at San Gabriel Mission and they settled on Rancho Santa Gertrudes. In the ensuing years, Pacifico and Martina became the parents of thirteen children and the family line carries all the way into modern Fullerton lore. Juan Pacifico's fourth child, Maria de los Dolores, married José Antonio Prudencio Yorba, son of Don Bernardo Yorba . . . one of their daughters, Angelina Yorba— Pacifico's granddaughter—married Samuel Kraemer . . . one of the

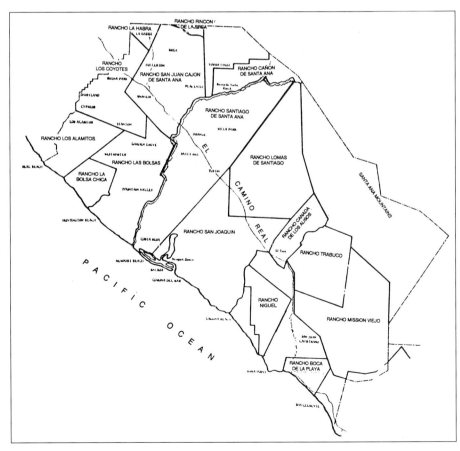

The ranchos of Orange County, including the nearly 36,000-acre Rancho San Juan Cajon de Santa Ana granted to Juan Pacifico Ontiveros, are depicted on this map. The Ontiveros rancho included the lands where the cities of Anaheim, Fullerton, Placentia, and Brea are now located. Map compiled by the author using several sources, but principally one prepared and copyrighted by First American Title Insurance Company Santa Ana, California.

Maria and Juan Pacifico Ontiveros were own-ers of the 35,970-acre Rancho San Juan Cajon de Santa Ana, which included what is now the city of Fullerton. Photo courtesy of Launer Local History Room, Fullerton Public Library

Kraemer daughters, Adella—Pacifico's great-granddaughter—married Walter Muckenthaler, who built the home now housing the Muckenthaler Cultural Center. Of course, by virtue of the Yorba-Kraemer link, Adella Muckenthaler was also the great-granddaughter of Don Bernardo Yorba.

Pacifico, who could not read or write and depended upon others to transact written business for him, took up the rancho claim after his father's death. Some important papers have been lost and no formal record of a grant with survey and juridicial possession has been located. Yet, in a May 1835 petition, Pacifico indicated he had been granted the lands of *El Cajon de Santa Ana* and asked for more.

Again a long process of rights determination was initiated. There apparently was some ceding of land done on the part of José Nieto, and, in September 1837, possession of ten square leagues of land—later reduced to eight square leagues, or about 35,970 acres—was formally granted to Pacifico Ontiveros. This five-sided piece of land—Rancho *San Juan Cajon de Santa Ana*—would cover that area of a modern map extending along the Los Angeles County line on the north, then Rose Drive–Tustin Avenue on the east to the Santa Ana River, then along the river to Ball Road, which forms the south boundary as far as Magnolia, and along Magnolia as the western boundary to the Los Angeles County line. The Ontiveros family happily occupied this land, which some called *Peor es Nada*, or "good for nothing," but which later produced some of the finest grapes, walnuts, and oranges ever marketed.

As a matter of course, it was pretty quiet on the rancho with long days, starting at 3:00 a.m., spent tending the cattle. Men would eat a hearty meal upon arising and then not eat again until late afternoon. The men and women both wore their hair long, with the men braiding it and tucking it under head handkerchiefs which were often topped by oval, low-crowned brimmed hats. The women parted and braided their hair, first using ribbon to tie it and, later, high combs to hold their hair high above their head.

Business was a matter of hard work, a good memory, and trust among men. Because of lack of literacy, written records were virtually nonexistent. Accounts were kept with tally sticks and a man's word was gospel; there was no room for mistrust. And, it was not always dull; rancheros welcomed every opportunity to party. Even work-like endeavors like cattle roundups offered an opportunity to celebrate, and there were the weddings, and the fiesta and festival days of the church. Visits from family and friends called for celebrations on their own merit. The partying sometimes lasted for days of singing, dancing, food, and conversation—the carefree life so often depicted in pictures, paintings, and movies.

When the United States took control of California after the end of the Mexican War and signing of the Treaty of Guadalupe y Hidalgo in 1848, Pacifico Ontiveros, like all his land-grant counterparts, faced the formidable task of proving his claim to the land, which was initially denied by the United States Board of Land Commissioners. But the fight continued with witnesses including Bernardo Yorba, Abel Stearns, Augustus Langenberger (Pacifico's son-in-law), George Hansen (a surveyor and one of the founders of Anaheim), and many others well-respected in the area. A decree of the Southern District Court dated January 29, 1856, reversed the decision of the Land Commissioners and Pacifico's title was declared valid. On December 7, 1857, a mandate of the Supreme Court to the judge of the Southern District Court of California confirmed the Ontiveros claim, but it was not until May 21, 1877—after Pacifico's death on March 7 of that year—that President Rutherford B. Hayes signed the patent to the land.

In 1857, Pacifico was approached about selling some of his land by a group of German immigrants interested in growing grapes. The land, however, had no access to water so Ontiveros convinced Bernardo Yorba to sell him a strip of land just wide enough for an irrigation ditch at a price reported at $200. Eleven days later, on September 12, 1857, Ontiveros sold 1,165 acres for $2,330—throwing in rights to the ditch for an additional $10—to John Frohling and George Hansen. Those lands—which Pacifico Ontiveros allegedly said "wouldn't keep a goat"—were the foundation for what became the city of Anaheim and, "Never," said Mildred Yorba MacArthur in her book, *Anaheim—The Mother Colony*, "did one man give so much for so little to so many."

Pacifico moved to his ranch at Santa Maria and we do not know, for sure, what prompted that decision. We do know, however, that several years of severe drought hit the area in the early 1860s (the rancho received but four inches of rain in all of 1862), that the Gold Rush was coming to an end and that the Civil War was raging in the South. Of those, the drought may have been the principal factor that prompted Pacifico to (1) give to his sons Patricio and Juan Nicolás (Juanito)—for "natural love and affection"—3,900 acres of land at the southeast corner of the rancho (where Placentia was later founded) and (2) on the same day, May 22, 1863, sell the remaining rancho—30,672 acres, including those lands where Fullerton now stands—to Abel Stearns. The price was $6,000.

One year later, May 10, 1864, the Ontiveros brothers sold their 3,900 acres to their brother-in-law, Augustus Langenberger (married to María Petra de Jesus Ontiveros), and his partner, Benjamin Dreyfus, for $3,480. They, in turn, sold the land to Daniel Kraemer on April 27, 1865, for $4,600—when, as historian Virginia Carpenter says in *Placentia, A Pleasant Place to Live*, "the story of Placentia itself really begins."

The Abel Stearns story is a different one altogether.

Don Abel Stearns—whom historian Robert Glass Cleland calls "The Personification of an Age," in his *The Cattle on a Thousand Hills*—was a Massachusetts native who took first to the sea and then moved to Mexico where he became a naturalized citizen. He came to California in 1829, first to Monterey and then to the pueblo of Los Angeles where he established himself as a merchant. He built a successful business and began expanding, specifically into a warehouse in San Pedro where he became the leading trader with merchantmen and rancheros.

Stearns had differences with some of the state's political leaders and with some of those with whom he traded, in one instance suffering severe stab wounds that disfigured his face and permanently impaired his speech. But, for the most part, he got along well with people and made an especially good friend of one of Southern California's most influential rancheros and politicos, Don Juan Bandini. Their relationship was further cemented when Stearns married one of Bandini's five daughters, Arcadia. He was forty years of age, she was fourteen, and their marriage endured until Stearn's death in 1871.

In 1842 Stearns began the land purchases that were to make him the baron of all land barons by buying Rancho Los Alamitos for $6,000. So well positioned was he by 1850—the county assessment for that year showed the rancho pastured 10,000 head of cattle, 700 horses, and 1,100 sheep—that John C. Fremont offered him $300,000 for Rancho Los Alamitos, a deal which Stearns turned down.

By 1862 Stearns had acquired over 200,000 acres in the Los Angeles–San Bernardino area and, although he continued to acquire properties—including

Don Bernardo Yorba followed in the footsteps of his father, José Antonio Yorba, and obtained his own rancho in the north part of what was to become Orange County. Don Bernardo, Jose's third son, made much of his Rancho Cañon de Santa Ana—and Rancho Sierra (Riverside County) and Rancho Rincón (San Bernardino County) which he purchased later—becoming, according to the 1850 California census, one of the three richest men residing in what was to become Orange County. Don Bernardo died in 1858 at the age of fifty-seven. Photo courtesy of Launer Local History Room, Fullerton Public Library

A way station for travelers to the Yorba rancho, the structure known as "Coyote House" was located in the hills north of what is now Fullerton Municipal Airport. The home—some have said the Yorbas built it in about 1850, others claim it was built by the Robinson Trust as a place for potential land purchasers to stay—was a landmark for the pioneering settlers of the area. Photo Courtesy of Launer Local History Room, Fullerton Public Library

the Fullerton lands—a drop in cattle prices caused by an overstocked market sent him slipping into a financial sinkhole—and then the severe drought of 1862–1864 left his lands parched and cattle dying. Southern California was no longer "the pastoral scene of grazing cattle as far as the eye could see," described by Esther Cramer in *La Habra, The Pass Through The Hills*, but rather a dry and barren plain swept by hot Santa Ana winds and strewn with the bones of thousands of dead cattle.

Stearns alone lost 30,000 head of cattle—including many he slaughtered for the hides and tallow—and he sank deeper and deeper into debt and found

Abel Stearns was a native of Salem, Massachusetts, who became a naturalized citizen of Mexico before venturing to California in 1829. A successful Los Angeles merchant who solidified his political status with marriage to the daughter of Juan Bandini, he was destined to become the area's largest landowner, controlling more than two hundred thousand acres of valuable Southern California properties by the early 1860s, including the former Ontiveros Rancho and the acreage upon which Fullerton now stands. Stearns died in 1871. Photo from an engraving in The Cattle on a Thousand Hills, *by Robert Glass Cleland, The Huntington Library, San Marino, California, 1951*

lawsuit upon lawsuit being filed against him. He gained temporary relief with a loan in 1868, but, facing more trouble after those funds ran out, was forced to join with Alfred Robinson, Sam Brannan, Edward F. Northam, Charles B. Polhemus, and Edward Martin in formation of a trust designed to subdivide and sell the Stearns holdings. The Robinson Trust, as it was called, covered 177,796 acres of land—nearly 278 square miles—including what was to become Fullerton.

It was with agents of the Trust—in fact, often with Stearns himself—that the pioneer settlers of Fullerton would often deal.

This picture of the Alexander Gardiner family at their West Orangethorpe Avenue ranch was probably taken after the turn of the century. Alex Gardiner (with the beard) strikes a familiar pose at the right in the picture. Photo courtesy of Launer Local History Room, Fullerton Public Library

CHAPTER V

The Pioneers

1860 – 1880

"Pathfinder of the Pioneers" is the title given to Jedediah Strong Smith, the trailblazing American mountain man, by historian Robert Glass Cleland in his *From Wilderness to Empire, A History of California*, 1542–1900, published in 1944. Cleland said Smith and other Rocky Mountain fur trappers, "were the pioneers of all Far Western frontiersmen, the trailblazers for subsequent explorers, the pathfinders of the course of empire to the western sea," and, while Fullerton pioneers did not, for the most part, follow the same route "blazed" by these men, it was their success in doing so, and tales of it, that inspired the western movement.

Jedediah Smith led the first party that, in 1826, crossed the mountains into California and visited at San Gabriel Mission in November of that year. It is very likely he traveled the mission trail through Fullerton at the end of that year. But Spanish authorities were not at all pleased with his presence. Historian Maurice S. Sullivan, in his 1934 *The Travels of Jedediah Smith*, explained that "From San Gabriel Jedediah Smith rode down to San Diego to meet Governor José María de Echeandia, by whom he was received with polite suspicion." Smith returned to San Pedro by boat, bought some horses, and, under orders, left San Gabriel Mission on January 17, 1827, ostensibly headed out of California the way he came in. In fact, however, he made a left turn after crossing the San Gabriel Mountains and headed into the San Joaquin Valley in search of beaver.

It was about forty years later that the first settlers actually came to what is now Fullerton. Certainly among the first was Domingo Bastanchury, a Basque sheepherder from the Pyrenees of France, who probably arrived sometime during the early 1860s. Daniel Kraemer settled on the lands to the east of the city, in the "Placentia District," in 1865, and pioneers of the "Orangethorpe District" of Fullerton—Stones, Burdorfs, Rordens, Boeckmans, and Gardiners among them— came on the scene in 1868 and 1869. As we review their stories—and those of pioneers who arrived in the 1870s, the Porters, Sansinenas, des Granges, and Gilmans—we should remember the townsite, indeed, the very name *Fullerton*, was still a decade or two in the future.

Domingo Bastanchury, called "The Father of Fullerton" in one early history, was born in Aldudes, Basses-Pyrenees, France, in 1839. The son of Gracian

Domingo Bastanchury arrived in the Fuller-ton area in the early to mid-1860s, where he invested his accumulated savings in a lease negotiated with Abel Stearns for land on which to run his herd of sheep. From an engraving by Campbell Brothers in Samuel Armor's History of Orange County California, Historic Record Company, Los Angeles, 1921

The former Maria Oxarart married Domingo Bastanchury in Los Angeles on July 16, 1874, and took over much of the formal dealings of the Bastanchury operations. She died at the family home on Las Palmas Avenue on the evening of January 1, 1943. From an engraving by Campbell Brothers in Samuel Armor's History of Orange County California, *Historic Record Company, Los Angeles, 1921*

Bastanchury was perhaps of noble ancestry with a lineage dating back to the fifteenth century, according to a granddaughter, Mrs. Angelo R. Ferraris, whose recollections were told by Clyde Snyder in a three-part 1957 *Los Angeles Times* series. Domingo had no formal educational training, working very hard every day in his homeland to learn the trades of sheepherding and fishing. Hearing of the opportunity in America, especially in California on the heels of the Gold Rush, he decided to take a look for himself and set sail on a working six-month voyage which ended with his arrival in San Francisco on October 12, 1859.

Domingo turned to his old trade and began to stockpile savings while working as a shepherd in various California locations, ever inching southward and eventually getting his own herd of sheep. Some say this odyssey lasted ten years, others report it was much less and he may have arrived here as early as 1860. His decision to permanently settle in the Fullerton area may have occurred about the same time as the formation of the Robinson Trust in May of 1868. That's because his leasing of the lands—at ten cents per head of sheep, per year—from Abel Stearns drew the ire of other trust members, who said Stearns was not authorized to lease the property. One history of the Jerome B. Stone family indicates that the Bastanchurys were here when the Stones arrived in 1868.

Spurred by a demand for wool created by the cotton shortages resulting from the Civil War and the Reconstruction Period which followed, Domingo Bastanchury went on to purchase his own land and build the largest herd of sheep in the area, estimated at between ten and twenty thousand head.

"The most desolate, lonesome place in the world," is what Mrs. Domingo Bastanchury said of the Fullerton where she came to live after her marriage on July 16, 1874. She was born Maria Oxarart in 1848 to Basque farmers in the same province where Domingo was born and raised. They settled in North Fullerton, their adobe ranch house being located about where the Fullerton Municipal Golf Course clubhouse is now. Mrs. Bastanchury, after a year of study, took over the recordkeeping and much of the formal business dealings of the ranch. She said there were only two homes between hers and Los Angeles and that she was the only woman in the area. She often went weeks, while her husband was out with the shepherds, without seeing another white person.

The couple had four sons—Dominic J., born in 1881; Gaston, 1884; Josef, 1887; and John, 1889—who later played key roles in converting the ranch to citrus crops. Domingo died in 1909 at the beautiful family home he had built in 1906 on what became Las Palmas Avenue, but, under the direction of his wife and sons, the ranch continued to prosper. The great artesian springs which produce the clear waters distributed to this day by the Bastanchury Water Company, were first tapped in 1914. In the late teens and early 1920s the ranch's conversion to citrus began. At one time the ranch lands were host to what was called the largest citrus ranch in the world, twenty-seven hundred acres in oranges and lemons whose fragrance wafted over motorists traveling "the State Highway"—Harbor Boulevard—that passed by the row upon row of fruit-bearing trees. At the outset of the citrus conversion, the Bastanchury's had planted tomatoes between the trees in order to have some revenue-producing crops while waiting for the trees to bear fruit. Gaston Bastanchury reported in a 1926 *Fullerton News-Tribune* story that, "During part of the present tomato season we were shipping one-third of the entire output of the state of California" and, "Right now our shipments represent one-half of the state total. At the peak these shipments have run as high as 15 cars per day."

This photo is identified as the "Kraemer Adobe," but is believed to originally be the home of the Pacifico Ontiveros family. Photo courtesy of Launer Local History Room, Fullerton Public Library

Sheep, water, tomatoes, oranges, and lemons do not tell the entire story of the Bastanchury Ranch; there were also dairy herds—"more than 100 milk cows . . . renowned for (their) output of pure rich milk" according to a 1909 *Pictorial American* story—and hogs—"there are fattened there constantly an average of 1,000 hogs"—and beef cattle "running into the hundreds." And there is the matter of oil, a somewhat touchy subject in Bastanchury lore. It seems, according to the recollections of the late Judge Raymond Thompson in a *California State University, Fullerton, Oral History Program* interview by Gerald M. Welt, that the Murphy Oil Company leased Bastanchury property to look for oil. A well was

Andrew Rorden farmed an area to the northeast of the townsite which became the site of Fullerton College. He is seen here inspecting the property in a photo taken in about 1880, according to local historians. Photo courtesy of Launer Local History Room, Fullerton Public Library

drilled and oil found, but the Bastanchurys were told there was no oil and the well was plugged. Later, the company came back, said there were some clay deposits it was interested in, bought three thousand acres for about $60 per acre—and began to pull out the oil. Some ten or twelve years later, the Bastanchury sons became aware of the incident and filed a suit for $72 million, claiming fraud. Judge Thompson said that, because of the time element and delay in filing action, the family settled for about $1.2 million. This money, combined with $2.5 million in bonds sold by the Bastanchury Ranch Company, helped finance the conversion to citrus and other ranch development.

The Tidings Catholic newspaper

Jerome B. Stone came to the lands which became Fullerton in 1868, the first of the West Orangethorpe Avenue settlers. Mr. Stone's bulk (248 pounds) was well publicized, and is verified by the photograph (he's seated in a chair by the tree in the center of the photo). Photo courtesy of Launer Local History Room, Fullerton Public Library

in 1925 termed Mrs. Bastanchury "a prominent Catholic" and reported "it is due to her generosity that the present church at Fullerton [St. Mary's] was built, she being the donor of the site, as well as the main altar." She died at the ranch home on East Las Palmas the evening of January 1, 1943, some sixty-nine years after coming to the barren, now bustling, Fullerton lands.

In 1865, Daniel Kraemer, a Bavarian native who had settled in Illinois early in the 1840s, made a trip to California at the urging of friends. He had the opportunity to purchase the thirty-nine hundred acres from August F. Langenberger, paying $4,600 cash on April 27, 1865, according to Virginia Carpenter in *Placentia, A Pleasant Place to Live*. He returned to Illinois, visited again in 1866, then gathered his family to make the permanent move in 1867.

Kraemer settled in on the old rancho, moving his family into the dirt-floored Ontiveros adobe, and began farming. It would be years before these lands produced another "crop"—oil—which forever changed the life of the entire community.

About the same time the Kraemers were settling in, another family arrived on the scene some five miles to the southwest. Jerome B. Stone and his wife, Anna, had traveled by ox team from Iowa to California in 1856, settling first in Alameda in the northern part of the state where they had a successful farming operation. When he loaded up the wagon and pointed the oxen south in 1868, he had three thousand dollars in his pocket and was looking for some good land to buy. He found it at the northwest corner of Spadra (Harbor) and Orangethorpe, and he purchased—for ten dollars per acre—two hundred acres that extended westward and as far north as where the Santa Fe tracks were later to run.

The family, after first living in the adobe "Coyote House," built their home "on the back part of the land, about where West Maple Street (Valencia) is now," according to one family history, which also claims this was the first house built in what is now Fullerton. The Stones set to farming, and, as it turned out, it was a good thing they had a cash reserve. The first year the grain crop was washed out in a flood; the second year drought cut drastically into production; and the third year it was grasshoppers, which, besides destroying the crop, "even ate the harnesses off the horses, and their saddles."

Later, though, the family enjoyed big success with grapes and walnuts and then oranges. Jerome B. Stone played an active role in the community, joining in building an irrigation ditch to supply water to Orangethorpe area residents. A humorous story about Stone and the irrigation ditch was told by Nina May Miller, granddaughter of Henry Burdorf, another pioneer. In her words: "A laughable incident occurred in this connection one day. A breakout occurred, and several men rushed to the scene, but for a time were unable to do nothing [sic], for as soon as a dam was built the water would seep under. So finally Mr. Stone, who was rather fat, lay down across the ditch and the sand was piled on him. The runaway water was stopped and Mr. Stone suffered no ill-effects." A note in the *Fullerton Tribune* on May 27, 1893, bears out the story of Mr. Stone's bulk: "J. B. Stone, who lives a mile south of town, has 33 acres in hard shell walnut trees twelve years old, which are looking fine. Mr. Stone has been living here twenty-five years, and weighs 248 pounds and his wife 216 pounds. How is that for Fullerton climate?"

In the year of the grasshoppers, 1871, a daughter, Martha Elenora—appropriately nicknamed "Grasshopper"—was born to Jerome B. and Anna Stone, a birth which appears to be the first of a non-Indian child on the lands now

"In 1869, this section of the country was very dreary, dry desert land filled with plants such as cactus, castor bean, sage brush, elderberry trees, and in some places mustard; and animal life such as quail, jackrabbits, doves, coyotes, and even wildcat," wrote Nina May Miller, granddaughter of Henry Burdorf who came to the land first known as Orangethorpe and then as Fullerton in 1869. His family is pictured in the 1880s. Photo courtesy of Launer Local History Room, Fullerton Public Library

The Alexander Gardiner family is seen at their homestead on West Orangethorpe Avenue where they settled in 1869 and operated a successful walnut ranch after migrating from Tennessee. Photo courtesy of Launer Local History Room, Fullerton Public Library

John R. Gardiner was born in the West Orangethorpe Avenue ranch home of his father Alexander in 1873 and the hardworking young man was elected to Fullerton's first City Council in 1904—an oddity in that one could hardly have expected that a native son would serve on the city's first governing board. Photo courtesy of Launer Local History Room, Fullerton Public Library

contained within Fullerton, although that subject has been the center of considerable debate over the years. Martha Stone became Mrs. H. C. Babize and she and her husband were very active in music circles during the early years of the century. Also, it is she to whom we are indebted for some of the word pictures, like the following, of early-day Fullerton. "Firewood was scarce on the fertile plain but the mustard grew so large that the stalks were cut and burned in cookstoves and for heating," Martha Babize told one interviewer. "When these were not available the ranchers hitched their teams to the farm wagons and journeyed up to Carbon Canyon where oil seepage from the ground could be cut in chunks and the 'brea' hauled back to be used for fuel. . . . Little did they realize the potential value of that oil seepage in those days. . . ." For many years Mrs. Babize lived at 123 East Amerige Avenue in a cottage with a dining room window containing leaded panes of glass she said were from the St. George Hotel, one of the first buildings in downtown Fullerton and the scene of "many pleasurable parties" in her youth.

Jerome B. Stone was among those who had written to William M. McFadden, a well-educated Pennsylvanian who had come to Northern California in about 1864, and urged his move to this area. McFadden decided to join his fellow Masons, including also John Hanna, J. K. Tuffree (a son-in-law of C. B. Polhemus of the Robinson Trust), and Albert Clark, who had settled in the Anaheim area. He arrived in Anaheim on Christmas Day, 1868, and, in his own words, set out "in quest of cheap land on which to build a home and plant an orange orchard."

McFadden's daughter, Carrie McFadden Ford (she married Fullerton's first grocer, Herbert Ford), later told how her father carried his "quest" northeast of Anaheim, to Crowther's Corner (Placentia and Chapman Avenues), where he liked the sturdy look of the mustard but learned from the Robinson Trust that the property was spoken for. He went a bit further north, to the vicinity of what is now Placentia Avenue and Yorba Linda Boulevard, and there found the land of his choice. On January 4, 1869, he bought ninety-one acres for $10 per, paying one-quarter ($228) down with the balance due in three annual installments.

This grouping of photos includes Mr. and Mrs. Richard Hall Gilman, the plaque commemorating the planting of the first commercial valencia orange grove on Gilman's property in 1880 and a picture of the Gilman homestead on the west wide of Placentia Avenue. Photo courtesy of Launer Local History Room, Fullerton Public Library

McFadden later said, "I found I could not complain of at its cost . . . but I soon discovered that what at first sight appeared cheap was quite dear." He explained: "No lumber nearer than San Pedro and cost there $30 per thousand for rough lumber, $20 more for hauling it out. All kinds of produce very dear—barley 2 cents per pound, lard 20 cents, can of axle grease 40 cents, etc. So my small purse of money soon dwindled until it became very attenuated."

While William McCormick McFadden was definitely a Placentian, he played a very large role in several aspects of Fullerton growth. His advice was sought on school matters, he was present at the organization of the Chamber of Commerce in 1895 (in fact, was elected to the board, a position he resigned the following week), and was very active in water supply issues. He also was one of five commissioners named to organize the new Orange County, which his son Ralph would later serve as a supervisor for many years.

It was also in 1869 that more families began moving into the "Orangethorpe District." This included a group of German farmers who had come to San Francisco a year earlier—Henry Burdorf, Chris Rorden, and Henry Boeckman. Once in this area they joined to purchase a quarter section of land, 260 acres, on East Orangethorpe for ten dollars per acre. Mr. Burdorf's share was 100 acres. Nina May Miller, who said she got information for her story *Early Days in Fullerton* from her grandmother, Mrs. Dorothea Burdorf; from B. F. Porter (an 1870 pioneer settler of whom we will hear later); and from Mrs. Carrie McFadden Ford, tells us one of the reasons these early settlers were willing to give up everything in their homeland to face the hardships and uncertainties of a new country was lack of opportunity. She explained: "the law of primogeniture still held good in Europe. This meant that the oldest son received the entire inheritance and yet the younger were obligated to care of their parents in their old age. America offered a greater chance for a successful, independent livelihood than their homeland to these younger brothers."

However, when they arrived here, they may have been disheartened, for "this section of the country was very dreary dry desert land filled with plants such as cactus, castor bean, sagebrush, elderberry trees, and in some places mustard—and animal life such as quail, jackrabbits, doves, coyotes, and even wildcats." Her story of early hardships was similar to that told by Mrs. Babize; she said that in the year of the grasshoppers Henry Burdorf had a fine crop, but after the insects struck "by nightfall not a spear of grain, not a grape, not anything was left." She also told of the grape blight that wiped out the wine industry in Anaheim and the Orangethorpe area: "All the grapes in the country around died, although two months earlier they were healthy looking and promised a good crop. Many prohibitionists take the credit of having brought on this blight through prayer, but I fear very few of the earliest pioneers appreciated their work."

One of the more interesting tales in the Miller story concerns the providing of water to the area. It was in 1872, she said, that "Mr. Porter, Mr. Burdorf, Mr. Rorden and Mr. Boeckman, together with eight or ten other men, decided that they must have water. . . . So the men decided to dig a ditch to be called the Farmer's ditch [others say it was called the North Anaheim ditch] from the Yorba supply to the Anaheim ditch. The ditch fell into disuse after a few wet years, but, in 1880, was again needed and a complete rebuilding job—with a flume—was required. Burdorf and Porter made up a committee that raised three hundred dollars to pay for the wood and the new ditch and flume were completed in 1881. Benjamin Franklin Porter later was successful in working out a contract with the

José Sansinena came from the same Basque province as Domingo Bastanchury, arriving in California in 1872 and soon entering Bastanchury's employ. Sansinena married Dolores Ordoqui at the Plaza Church in Los Angeles in 1889 and soon thereafter purchased five thousand acres in the La Habra valley where he continued raising sheep. The Sansinenas invested in Fullerton's business future with property on the south side of the 100 block of East Commonwealth Avenue, a structure which for a time housed the community's grammar school. José Sansinena died in May 1895, but his widow and four children continued operations at the ranch for many years, even after Mrs. Sansinena became Mrs. Ysidoro Eseverri. Photo courtesy of Launer Local History Room, Fullerton Public Library

Fullerton's first settlers located in an area which was originally known as "North Anaheim" along Orangethorpe Avenue, mostly west of Spadra Road (Harbor Boulevard) and extending to what is now Brookhurst Road. These pioneers of the late 1860s first sent their children to Anaheim schools, and then to Orangethorpe School after that district was organized (Louis Plummer says this occurred in 1872). This group of students is seen outside the wood-sided school building in a picture taken about 1880. Photo courtesy of Launer Local History Room, Fullerton Public Library

Yorbas whereby the Yorbas would only draw water during daytime hours and the settlers were able to take water at night and fill reservoirs. Miss Miller said, "this meant hundreds of thousands of dollars to Fullerton."

Another 1869 arrival to the area was Alexander Gardiner. As J. M. Guinn wrote in *Historical and Biographical Record of Southern California* in 1902, "From a patch of ground whereon the mustard had been wont to flourish in uninterrupted luxuriance year after year, has developed, in the Fullerton district, the fine walnut property of Alexander Gardiner. As early as 1869 this pioneer migrated to California from his former home in Tennessee, and originally purchased one hundred and sixty acres of land. . . ."

A native of Scotland (born in Glasgow January 24, 1838), Gardiner came to America in 1855, his family settling first near Knoxville, Tennessee. He married Susan R. Reeder in 1864 and they were to have seven children, among them a daughter Jennie, who married Otto des Granges of another pioneer Fullerton family, and son John R., later elected to the very first Fullerton City Council (Board of Trustees). Alexander Gardiner was one those growers and shippers who promoted and incorporated the Fullerton Walnut Growers' Association and, said Guinn, "From the thrift and order and general air of prosperity noticeable in the home and surroundings of Mr. Gardiner, it would seem that he has realized many of his expectations in coming to California. Be that as it may, he has won the esteem and confidence of all who are fortunate enough to know him, and is considered one of the county's most substantial and reliable citizens."

One of the first 1870s immigrants in this area was Benjamin Franklin Porter, a native of Tennessee who was raised in Texas before coming via wagon train to Fullerton in 1870. Porter added his observations to a diary of the 1869–1870 journey kept by the wagonmaster's daughter, Sarah Keener. The trip ended at Los Nietos on February 14, 1870, and Porter subsequently purchased forty acres of land on the north side Orangethorpe Avenue, west of Euclid Avenue, where he and his wife raised fifteen children. Mrs. Porter's parents, the E. S. Meads, purchased property across the street.

Copies of title registrations on the Porter land on file at the Fullerton Public Library Launer Local History Room include the original patent (May 1877) on the land issued to Juan Pacifico Ontiveros. On the land adjacent to the Porters, a man named John Kerr built a home in 1882—later owned by the Almon Goodwins, then the Greenoughs, and then, from 1919 to 1984, by Benjamin Franklin Porter's son, Rufus, and grandson, Stanley—which is now recognized as the oldest extant house in Fullerton (since the Otto des Granges home was dismantled). The home, generally known as the "Porter House," is located at 771 West Orangethorpe Avenue and is used today by a social services agency after serving many years as a restaurant.

Benjamin Franklin Porter was very active in his chosen community, including helping form the Orangethorpe School in 1872 and Fullerton High School in 1893, and in water distribution matters, starting, as we have read, in helping dig the Farmer's ditch. Later he helped direct the Anaheim Union Water Company, was active in Democratic politics and in banking, serving at the time of his death as a director of the Fullerton branch of the Security–First National Trust and Savings Bank. After his death in 1941—at the family home on Orangethorpe where he and his wife celebrated their seventy-second anniversary earlier that year—his obituary in the *Fullerton News-Tribune* read, in part "He had been active throughout his life in the development of this district. Its first roads, first high school, irrigation systems and walnut marketing co-operatives all benefitted by his wise and willing counsel. . . . His energy and vision have played an important part in the progress of the community in which he chose to make his home."

Further east, out near the "Placentia District," there was also pioneering activity of significance. In 1873, Otto des Granges, a native of Prussia, Germany, the eighth child in a family that fled France during the Huguenot uprising, purchased eighty acres of land bounded by State College Boulevard and Acacia Avenue on the east and west respectively and by Chapman Avenue and Commonwealth Avenue on the north and south. The property was devoted first to general farming and later to walnut and orange production, "in the cultivation of which he accomplished satisfactory results," according to one early history. Ranch access was off Acacia and the family built the home at 2000 East Wilshire Avenue—once known as the "oldest in Fullerton." The southwest quarter of the property plays host to Ladera Vista Junior High.

Otto des Granges died in 1898, but left behind a family—his widow, Josephine, and children John C., Joseph P., Otto, and Mrs. C. W. Crall—that carried on for many years the family traditions, which, a 1902 history written by J. M. Guinn, said, "reached into remote European history."

Not too far away from des Granges was a ranch operated by Richard Hall Gilman, a New Hampshire native who had worked his way as a "ship's boy" to California in 1862, where he began his business career as a dishwasher. But, his promise was recognized by a group of Healdsburg ranchers anxious to explore the potential of citrus ranching in Southern California and they sent Gilman on a mission. He returned north after purchasing 110 acres of land on the west side of Placentia Avenue extending to State College Boulevard, paying $17.50 per acre for the property in October 1872. This land was destined to house the first commercial Valencia orange grove and, many years later, the campus of California State University, Fullerton.

Gilman's associates formed the Southern California Semi-Tropical Fruit Company (later named the Placentia Fruit Company) and sent Gilman back to manage their investment. On January 1, 1873, he enthusiastically set about clearing the land of cacti, sagebrush, and willows, digging a well and setting out seedling oranges, planting grapevines and walnut trees, and building a home. His daughter, Helen Gilman Bowen, tells us about the ranch in her 1978 book, *Mt. Shasta or Bust*, a delightfully descriptive diary of the family's lengthy 1890s Northern California journey:

"*. . . Pomegranates wound a big horsehoed yard where grass billowed so deeply that children could hardly navigate. Cypress swooped from out of the shoe to a willowed ditch, forbidden. It was the terror of every mother living along Placentia Avenue. Pampas grass and date palms alternately sidled inward the shoe, westward toward the house where all was so overgrown that only the company front porch nosed into the shoe. Dark red roses ran along the walk that centered the yard. Among them were narcissus that, with winter rains, set yellow cups to white saucers. In the spring, blue iris joined the roses. Peacocks paraded . . . a double row of English walnuts . . . lined the driveway, coming in from the east off Placentia Avenue and centering through the length of the ranch to Cypress Street [State College Boulevard].*"

It was to this scene that Gilman introduced the Valencia orange in 1880, and at a ceremony in March 1934—complete with orange juice toasts—the Native Daughters of the Golden West placed a plaque (later moved from near Placentia Avenue to a planter in the quad of CSUF).

Before closing this chapter, we should note that not all the pioneers made the trek westward at the urging of friends or relatives, as was the case in most instances cited here. Some were enticed by the advertising of the land companies, including the Los Angeles and San Bernardino Land Company (more often called the Stearns Rancho Company) formed by the Robinson Trust to subdivide and sell the Abel Stearns properties. Not all propaganda distributed by the land speculators held up to firsthand observation, as witnessed by the following report on an 1869 incident from historian J. M. Guinn, as quoted by Esther Cramer in *La Habra: The Pass Through The Hills*:

"*. . . just before we cast loose from the wharf at San Francisco an active young man came aboard the steamer with an armful of boom literature, the first I had seen. It was maps, plots and circulars descriptive of the lands of the Los Angeles and San Bernardino Land Company [the Stearns ranches]. These he distributed where he thought they would do the most good. A map and description of the city of Savana [sic] fell to my lot. The city was described as located on a gently sloping mesa overlooking the valley of Santa Ana. Sites had been reserved by its founders for churches and schools and a central location was held in reserve for a city hall. A few weeks after my arrival I visited the city. I found it on the western slope of the*

Coyote Hills, about six miles north of Anaheim. Long solitary rows of white stakes marked the line of its streets. A solitary coyote on a round top knoll, possibly the site of the prospective city hall, gazed despondently down the street upon the debris of a deserted sheep camp. The other inhabitants of the city of Savana [sic] had not arrived, nor have they to this day put in an appearance."

Mrs. Cramer notes: "The white stakes of the ghost town of Savanna have long since disappeared. The sites of the future schools and churches lie under the greens and fairways of the Los Coyotes Country Club, and the bulldozers have pushed the round top knoll, the possible city hall site, into residential lots. . . ."

There were others among the 1860s and 1870s pioneers who played major roles in area development—like José Sansinena, who, in 1872, joined Bastanchury in tending sheep, became a partner, and then acquired his own land and established a dynasty in the hills of La Habra before acquiring a business block in downtown Fullerton. But those cited herein are among the principles, this area's trailblazing pioneers, people who tended to keep to themselves, working to establish a foothold within their individual "districts"—Orangethorpe, Placentia, Anaheim. There was no "Fullerton."

It was they who initiated productive use of these lands; they who dug the ditches that delivered water to the rich but parched soil; they who set the pace for fortitude and patience, hard work and education; they who endured the hardships and stayed the course of settlement. And though the townsite was later established in a location away from the early pioneers "who had done the most to start Fullerton," the settlers were not unhappy. Nina May Miller expressed their feelings clearly in her paper, *Early Days in Fullerton,* "the old pioneers did not mind this. Living to see the fruits of their work was reward enough for them."

They had set the stage for the founders and builders who followed.

This home, built by rancher John Kerr in 1882, is still standing today at 771 West Orangethorpe Avenue where it is in use by a social service agency after serving for several years as a restaurant. It is most commonly known as "The Porter House" because members of that family occupied the residence from 1919 to 1984. Photo courtesy of Launer Local History Room, Fullerton Public Library

CHAPTER VI

The Founders

1880-1900

"The land was so fertile . . . they wanted their own land and they came," one local history noted in what most would agree is an oversimplified explanation for the westward movement. But "they" certainly did come to settle Fullerton's mustard covered plains . . . in response to land company advertising; for the health of loved ones; at the beckoning of friends or relatives. And they stayed, so great was the promise, in spite of nature's hurdles—flood, drought, fire—adding burdens to their work-aching shoulders. They arrived with vision, and patience, and perseverance . . . and they prevailed.

In 1880 a disastrous fire swept across much of the Fullerton plain, "The Santa Ana wind blew a shepherd's fire so that it caught the grain stubble. . . . The fire passed Henry Hetebrink's place where it burned all the livestock and domestic animals. When it got as far as Orangethorpe, it caught Boeckman's haystack and from there burned their barn and house. They were able to save one rocking chair, a bed, a sewing machine, and a few clothes. Burdorf's haystack caught but the barn and house were saved by fresh grapes. Their haystack smoldered for nearly two weeks or until the first rain of the season came. Rordens lost everything . . . ," Nina May Miller wrote in *Early Days in Fullerton*. "Those whose things were burned were helped as much as possible by neighbors and friends. Anaheimers, too, were not too hard-hearted to help out. In due time enough money was gotten together to build a shack for them, but since few pioneers had any money, the immediate gifts were mostly household necessities and clothing."

Two years later, 1882, the Alexander McDermont family's wagon topped a hill on the northwest side of town and Grace McDermont Ford recalled what she saw:

"When we reached the brow of the hill, just north of what is now City Airport, my father told us that now we could see our new home. I was 8 years old but I will never forget the feeling of bewilderment that came over me as I saw this vast field of dry mustard, outlined now and then by a few gum trees and a rough house on Orangethorpe."

"In the annals of Fullerton, a name that will ever stand out distinctly in its history is that of Edward Russell Amerige, one of Orange County's foremost citizens," wrote Mrs. J. E. Pleasants in History of Orange County, California, *published in 1931. E. R. Amerige was born in Malden, Massachusetts, on August 1, 1857, and nearly thirty years later, on July 5, 1887, it was he who drove the first survey stake for the townsite of Fullerton in a field of mustard at what has become the intersection of Harbor Boulevard and Commonwealth Avenue. He died in Los Angeles on May 3, 1915. Photo courtesy of Launer Local History Room, Fullerton Public Library*

Alex McDermont bought sixty acres of the J. M. Guinn ranch, property bounded by (using current location) Euclid Street on the west, Brea Creek channel on the north, Woods Avenue on the east and the Santa Fe tracks on the south, where "The wild life was rather interesting . . . mountain lions, wildcats, coyotes, jack rabbits by the hundreds, squirrels, skunks, weasels. They all liked chickens so the chickens had to be very carefully housed."

McDermont became prominent in Fullerton civic circles, being among those who brought a newspaper to town and among the first subscribers to capital stock in the community's first bank. He also "used his influence" to help create the Fullerton Union High School; built a business block in downtown Fullerton (southwest corner of Harbor and Amerige); served as a director of the Placentia Orange Growers Association and of the water company; and was manager of the Walnut Growers Association. McDermont sold ten acres of his property to a brickmaker named Schindler for a brickyard on the south side of Commonwealth, another ten acres to

George Henry Amerige was the older of the brothers Amerige who founded the townsite of Fullerton. Born March 22, 1855, in Malden, Massachusetts, he and his brother—"founders of one of the most attractive and promising municipalities of Southern California,"—were "descendants of an old colonial family," according to Samuel Armor's Orange County history published in 1921. George Amerige and his wife Annette, who for many years lived in an apartment above the business building he built at the northeast corner of Commonwealth and Spadra (Harbor), were familiar figures in Fullerton where he died on December 1, 1947, at the age of ninety-two. Photo courtesy of Launer Local History Room, Fullerton Public Library

an A. Barrows, and five acres to F. R. Holcomb. When Schindler subsequently sold to James A. Vail, it meant that four Muscatine, Iowa, families—Holcombs, Vails, Barrowses, McDermonts—had been reunited as neighbors in Fullerton, according to the recollections of C. E. Holcomb, F. R. Holcomb's son.

It was also in 1882 (one account says 1883) that another family—brothers from Vermont via Michigan—settled in California. William L. and H. H. Hale "were at once attracted to the Fullerton-Placentia District" upon their arrival there in 1886, according to an accounting written in 1909. William settled in as foreman on the W. F. Botsford ranch before purchasing from Botsford a 28-acre tract. His home, erected in 1908, was described in 1909 as "among the show places of the . . . District and of Orange County." On East Chapman Avenue it is now home to a Montessori School. H. H. Hale lived for a time in Orange and Ontario and managed the Windemere Ranch of Andrew McNally before purchasing 20 acres in the Placentia area. He also developed holdings in the Beaumont and Delano areas while all the time being very active in the Fullerton Chamber of Commerce.

Four years after fire swept the plains, the lands were covered with water. In February 1884, rain fell like none had seen before—forty inches of rain in about ten days, is the way Mrs. Ford recalled it. "The land, which had been black loam clear to the hills, was covered with about a foot and a half of fine silt, as the Brea wash came over the ranch for the first time," she said in a 1945 *Daily News-Tribune* interview.

Founding Fullerton

Two years after the heavy rains a fateful visit to the area was made by two vacationing brothers from Malden, Massachusetts, successful hay and grain merchants who came west for some "duck shooting." Edward R. and George H. Amerige had visited first in Northern California in the summer of 1886, then ventured south to look over this area. They decided to invest in ten acres of land in Sierra Madre and settled in on the ranch home there. Visitors from the East persuaded the brothers to rent them the place for the winter, and the Ameriges headquartered at the Planters Hotel in Anaheim while going into the Westminster marshes to hunt. They decided they liked the area, seeing great potential for growth, so they sold the Sierra Madre ranch, sold some of their interests in Massachusetts, and moved lock, stock, and barrel to Anaheim, where they established a real estate office in the Albers Building.

"Driving out from Anaheim in all directions to shoot quail and dove, they became interested in what is now the Fullerton District and conceived and formulated a plan to start a town, thinking here, of all the places they had examined, would be the location for a successful and permanent municipality," George H. Amerige (stealing some of his verbiage from an earlier writing by his brother) said in a signed third-person paper entitled *Fifty Years in Fullerton* (April 1937). Edward R. Amerige had waxed poetic in *The Pictorial American and Town Talk* article (1909), giving a fanciful explanation for selecting these lands in one incredible sentence of about 200 words. He wrote:

"At the close of the great boom of 1886 and 1887, when Southern California was attracting the attention of the whole United States, and, I might say, civilized world; when people were flocking to Los Angeles and vicinity by the thousands, attracted by its wonderful and matchless climate and the possible resources of this, the new Mecca, for ambitious people of all climes—a land of peace, plenty and equitable climate excelled by no other; when cities sprang up like magic from wasteless and treeless plains; when by the advent of the eastern capitalist, who, with an abundance of enterprise and capital, made the supposed desert blossom and bloom like the rose; when, by the development of and use of water for irrigating purposes, a transformation scene was enacted that would equal 'the fairy tales of Aladdin'—two young tenderfeet, G. H. and E. R. Amerige, attracted by the rich and beautiful Fullerton-Placentia District, the accessibility and abundance of water for both domestic and irrigation purposes; after a thorough and careful inspection of all the surrounding country and many other locations, conceived and formulated the plan of starting a town, thinking that here, of all locations they had examined, would be the ideal location for a successful and permanent municipality."

Whatever the reason, the brothers decided here was the site they wanted. They purchased

George Herbert Fullerton was just forty-four years old when, as president of the land and development arm of the Santa Fe Railroad, made a decision to route the railroad's Los Angeles to San Diego line through a fledgling townsite set in a field of tall mustard. In turn, the railroad gained, free of charge, every "right of necessity". . . plus a half-interest in the townsite, and, in appreciation, the town was named Fullerton. George Fullerton was for many years postmaster in his hometown of Brockton, Massachusetts (then called North Bridgewater) where he was born August 5, 1843. He died in Los Angeles on January 29, 1929, at the age of eighty-six. Photo courtesy of Launer Local History Room, Fullerton Public Library

H. Gaylord Wilshire was an original investor in Fullerton, joining with Edward and George Amerige and the Pacific Land and Improvement Company in a May 1887 agreement to establish the townsite. Wilshire constructed (at a cost of about $8,000) the first business "block" in downtown Fullerton at the southeast corner of Spadra Road (Harbor Boulevard) and Commonwealth Avenue. Wilshire moved to Los Angeles where he enjoyed a flamboyant career, including politics, real estate development (including the Wilshire Tract, through which runs the now famed Wilshire Boulevard) and promotion of an electronic healing device he invented (which many called a fine example of "quackery"). Photo courtesy of Launer Local History Room, Fullerton Public Library

This photograph at the Edward Atherton home in East Fullerton was reportedly taken in July 1898, by newspaper editor Edgar Johnson. Edward Atherton is at left holding four-month-old Malcolm; Mrs. Edgar Johnson is in the center, seated high on the steps; and Mrs. Atherton is at the right. The animals are identified as field spaniels Fannie and Jack at the left and Berry, the mastiff, in front of Mrs. Atherton. Photo courtesy of Launer Local History Room, Fullerton Public Library

390 acres from brothers D. E. and C. S. Miles, followed by 20 acres from William S. Fish and another 20 acres from Joseph Frantz, creating a 430-acre, rectangular-shaped townsite. Using current names, the property was bounded approximately by Chapman Avenue on the north, Valencia Drive on the south, Raymond Avenue on the east, and Richman Avenue on the west. A copy of the agreement with the Miles brothers dated May 14, 1887, indicates the purchase price was "$68,250 gold coin" to be paid $5,000 at date of this agreement . . . $10,000 within 5 days after receipt of title . . . $15,000 in 6 months from the date hereof and the balance of $38,250 within 1 year from the date hereof." Deferred payments bore interest at the rate of 8 percent per annum and the Ameriges were, upon making the second payment, obligated to giving a promissory note for the remainder. The document was notarized by James C. Mackenzie on June 10, 1887, and filed with J. A. Fomay, Jr., deputy to Los Angeles County Recorder Frank A. Gibson, at 3:46 p.m. on that date.

Now, the Ameriges were confronted with the major issues of starting a town. Paramount to assuring its success were funding to pay off their obligations and the physical work of surveying, platting, and grading the land. George Amerige said in his third-person story:

> *"When they learned that the California Central Railroad Company, a subsidiary of the Santa Fe Railroad, would soon build a line from Los Angeles to San Diego, passing through Orange County [then, it was not yet a county] the Amerige Brothers waited on George H. Fullerton who, at that time, was president of the Pacific Land and Improvement Company and also the 'right-of-way' man for the railroad, who informed them that several surveys had been made, but none of them would take in their tract of land. By offering him a right-of-way through their land and an interest in the town-site, they prevailed upon him to change the survey to bring the railroad through their land and south into Anaheim."*

Thus, a giant step toward solving the problems had been taken. The financing issue was pretty well settled when, after receiving deeds and titles to the land, the Ameriges "proceeded to form a closed stock company, consisting of the Amerige Brothers, the Pacific Land and Improvement Company, and the Wilshire Brothers [the same ones for whom Wilshire Boulevard in Los Angeles is named], who paid a bonus to come into the company." The physical task was taken in hand when Frank Olmstead of Los Angeles was hired to survey and plot the site, and, according to George Amerige:

"On July 5, 1887, the first stake was driven in a field of mustard, at what is now the northeast corner of Commonwealth Ave. and Spadra Road by Edward R. Amerige. The building of the town and the selling of lots was on! The clearing of the land and grading of the streets was done by Fuller Brothers, of the Pioneer Transfer Company, Los Angeles."

Naming Fullerton

So, now there was a town—but it had no name. George Amerige said he and his brother declined to have the town named after them and it was they who suggested the name *Fullerton*, honoring the man who was bringing the railroad to town. However, it really was not quite that simple; the full story involves a vote in the absence of Mr. Fullerton, as well as a touch of humor. George Fullerton's son, Perry, told it this way at a 1947 meeting of Fullerton pioneers:

"Well, the way my father has always told it to me—I heard him tell it a number of times—was that they had laid out various towns around Southern California for the Santa Fe Railroad, and . . . they decided to put a town at this location, and when it came up to the question of a name, why the board of directors . . . wanted to name it for my father. My father said no, he didn't want to; he was a man who never wanted to put himself forward at all in the public eye, and he said no, he didn't care for that at all. So it was stopped right at that time . . . but he had to leave the vicinity for a few days and when he came back, why, the town was named Fullerton, and the President of the Santa Fe Railroad had okayed it, so that was all there was to it. "I guess that's about the whole story. Oh, yes, Mr. Smith, who was then President of the Santa Fe Railroad, wanted to name the town Marceline, after his wife, but the board members thought it sounded too much like vaseline, so they said no . . . so they went ahead and named it Fullerton."

With the city named, the Ameriges accepted the honor of naming the streets—*Malden* and *Highland* for the name of the town and the street, respectively, where they were born; *Amerige* for the family name; *Commonwealth* for

The Alexander McDermont family came to Fullerton in late 1882 after selling their farm in Iowa. The McDermonts became prominent in Fullerton circles, not only for their ranching efforts but for civic and business enterprise as well. McDermont built a big business building at the southwest corner of Spadra (Harbor) and Amerige in 1893, which, when it burned to the ground in a major fire in 1908, spurred formation of the Fullerton Fire Department. Photo courtesy of Launer Local History Room, Fullerton Public Library

This was the Fullerton residence of the McDermont family located on Nicholas (Euclid) near its intersection with Commonwealth Avenue, although neither street existed when the McDermonts bought the property in 1882. Photo courtesy of Launer Local History Room, Fullerton Public Library

This grand home was located at what became 311 West Commonwealth Avenue, now the location of the main branch of the Fullerton Public Library. Data at the Launer Local History Room of the library says the home was occupied by the McDermont family until 1908, then by the Gobar family until 1943 and, finally, by Dr. V. Rich until 1973 when the new library was constructed. Photo courtesy of Launer Local History Room, Fullerton Public Library

The family of Rev. F. R. Holcomb arrived via one of the very first trains to stop in Fullerton in September of 1888 and were met at the station by former and future neighbor Alexander McDermont, from whom they bought a portion of their Fullerton land. Their home, pictured here, was located at what is now 736 West Commonwealth Avenue. Photo courtesy of Launer Local History Room, Fullerton Public Library

"one of the finest avenues in Boston"; *Harvard (Lemon)* after the university; *Wilshire* for the brothers who joined in the Fullerton adventure; *Truslow* for the general ticket agent of the Santa Fe Railroad; *Northam (Chapman)* for Robert Northam, then agent for the Stearns Rancho Company (Robinson Trust); *Whiting* for Dwight Whiting, owner of the El Toro Ranch and a friend of the Ameriges; and *Spadra (Harbor)*, after a town near Pomona to which the "old trail" through Fullerton and Brea Canyon led.

Edward Amerige wrote in 1909: "The land was cleared, streets laid out and graded, business blocks started, and many dwellings were being erected and completed." The first structure was for the Ameriges, a small, wood-frame building where they "lived and transacted all their business of selling lots, etc." It was first located on the west side of south Spadra (Harbor) on the fifth narrow lot south of Commonwealth, but was moved several times about the downtown area in the early years. It remains with us today, at rest in Amerige Park behind the Senior Citizens Multi-Service Center.

Building Fullerton

George Amerige says he installed the town's first water system, "employing Chinamen to do the excavation work on the ditches. . . . Hooker Bros. supplied the water pipe and made the connections. . . . The first well was drilled by Padderatz Bros. [in the block bounded by Highland, Malden, Whiting and Wilshire Avenues] on September 26, 1887. . . . The first water was raised by an old fashion hot air engine and later by a windmill."

The first "significant" building—and an imposing one it was—was the St. George Hotel, an elaborate three-story facility set back from the northeast corner of Commonwealth and Harbor, about where the southwest portion of the block's interior parking lot is now located. Other structures soon followed, the first built by H. Gaylor Wilshire on two lots at the southeast corner of Harbor and Commonwealth, home of Fullerton's first grocery store (Ford and Howell) and later the famed Stern and Goodman general merchandise store; the next by C. Schindler, P. A. Schumacher, and T. S. Grimshaw—the center store becoming known as the Sansinena Block—on three East Commonwealth lots behind the Wilshire Build-

ing; followed by the Chadbourne Block on four lots at the northwest corner of Commonwealth and Harbor. Regarding the latter, George Amerige said, "The contractor, D. Gunning, left town in the night with the building unfinished and bills unpaid, so George Amerige, who was bondsman for him, paid the bills and finished the building." The Chadbourne Building, and that built by Schindler-Schumacher-Grimshaw, George Amerige said, were on lots given to the developers with the understanding that they would build business houses on them.

Through the years, differing stories have been told about the land company formed to "sell" Fullerton and what eventually became of it. Perhaps the most concise explanation was provided by George Amerige, when, in 1937, he wrote:

"The Wilshire Brothers purchased the Pacific Land and Improvement Company interest and the Fullerton Land and Trust Company came into existence. Failing to fulfill their contract with the Pacific Land and Improvement Company, their [Wilshire] holdings were taken over and they were dropped from the company. Then the Amerige Brothers and the Fullerton Land and Trust Company interests were segregated. This took place on April 4, 1890, and the Fullerton Land and Trust Company dissolved, the Pacific Land and Improvement Company selling and disposing of their interests and the Amerige Brothers staying with the town."

Some have said Fullerton grew out of a mid-1880s boom, but others dispute this, including the townsite founders. Edward Amerige said the founding of

A handwritten note on this photo labeled it: "Ditch line, now Spadra St., Fullerton, Cal., July 5, 1887." The note is signed, "Amerige Bros." One in a series entitled "Views of Fullerton" taken by "Shaffner, photographer, 500 Sixth Street, Los Angeles," it may have been used in promotional efforts for the new town of Fullerton. Photo courtesy of Launer Local History Room, Fullerton Public Library

In the early days the irrigation system was not just for providing life-giving water to crops, as these unidentified youngsters demonstrate in a "Greetings from Fullerton, Cal." postcard. Photo courtesy of Launer Local History Room, Fullerton Public Library

This is the "Cusick House" at 315 East Amerige Avenue, which was built in 1885 and at the time of this writing was undergoing a complete restoration. In one of Carrie McFadden Ford's stories about early Fullerton, she says, "The first dwellings were the house Mrs. Cusick lived in," and then goes on to describe several other homes in the townsite area. Photo courtesy of Launer Local History Room, Fullerton Public Library

Herbert Alvin Ford was Fullerton's first grocer and is the man who applied for and brought to Fullerton its first post office. In October of 1894, H. A. Ford came down with a severe case of pneumonia, his second bout with the disease in five years, and, according to Mrs. Ford, "passed away in three days." Photo courtesy of Launer Local History Room, Fullerton Public Library

Fullerton came "at the close" of the great boom, and George Amerige said, "Fullerton did not receive any natural benefit from the boom, for, before the advent of the railroad, the boom was over." Because storms washed out sections of roadbed, arrival of the first passenger train to Fullerton was delayed—until August 15, 1888, said George Amerige . . . until September 1888, said Edward Amerige. However, while the time of the first train's arrival may be debated, its effect is not: "the growth has been steady and conservative ever since, and the town has made remarkable progress and advancement," Edward Amerige wrote in 1909

More Settlers

As the townsite was developing, settlers continued to arrive. In the year of the town's creation, there came to the "southwest of the city" a man born in the French Alps near Grenoble who had enjoyed great success in the northern part of the state and, later, Whittier. Pierre Nicolas was forty-two when he came to Fullerton—"In those days . . . hardly more than a name"—and bought 131 acres on the east side of what is now Euclid Street (but was, for years, Nicolas—often misspelled as Nicholas—Avenue south of Valencia Drive. He came from East Whittier, where he had been engaged in cattle and sheep raising and general farming on a 1,700-acre property he sold for $80,000 (and which, a 1909 *Pictorial American* article said, "is today worth millions . . .").

Nicolas made his Fullerton ranch, "one of the most attractive places in Orange County," including, "a pleasing and commodius house" and grounds which "are beautiful indeed." He later acquired interests in the central part of Fullerton, at one time owning a busy hotel, and much of that property remains in the family to this date. He married Hypolite Vincente, his childhood sweetheart, bringing her from France for a Los Angeles wedding in June 1871. She died in 1899—"the great and lasting grief of Mr. Nicolas' life" after tragedy had been visited upon the family on January 5 of that year when two sons, Hilary J. and Martin A., aged fourteen and twelve, respectively, died in a cave-in at a gravel pit.

Another family which would leave a lasting impression on Fullerton arrived on the west side of town in September 1888. The F. R. Holcomb family came from Iowa on one of the Warner railroad "tourist excursions." C. E. Holcomb, son of F. R., recalled the event in a paper entitled *My Recollections Of The Early Days Of Fullerton, California*:

"We arrived in Los Angeles about 9 o'clock at night and we 'tourists' were permitted to remain in the cars until the next day. The next morning my father went to the ticket window in the Santa Fe Depot and asked for six tickets to Fullerton and when he looked at them they were for 'La Habra'. . . . the agent said the railroad station was La Habra but the townsite was called Fullerton. Later the railroad station was changed to Fullerton."

(Edward Amerige hinted there may have been some bitterness on the part of the railroad involved in the La Habra designation for Fullerton, explaining that George Fullerton had been "dispossessed of his title and interest in [the Pacific Land and Improvement Co.] and an attempt was made by the Santa Fe officials to change the name of Fullerton to La Habra; in fact, the first railroad tickets issued and sold to this point read, 'Los Angeles to La Habra,' and the name 'La Habra' was put upon the station, but the opposition to the change in the name was so great that the original name was restored.")

Holcomb's "recollections" are extensive, with descriptions of neighbors and friends, buildings and institutions, including local settlers such as Alexander McDermont, James A. Vail, John H. Clever, John Evans, a Mr. Williams, the Barrows and Sprague families, Henry Meiser, John P. Zeyn, William Schulte, C. Otto Rust, William Hetebrink, Andrew Rorden, Henry Schultz, Henry Kroeger, the Myerholtz family, H. Cahan, Pierre Nicolas, Lionel Browning, Sydmer Ross, Major Duffill, and the des Granges and Dauser families.

F. R. Holcomb—The Reverend F. R.—is credited with holding the first religious services on the townsite: "When we came a Sunday School that had been started by A. McDermont was moved to Fullerton and my father was asked to take charge of it and begin a Union preaching service. My father became superintendent of the Sunday School and began church services," C. E. Holcomb reports in *Early Days in Fullerton*, another paper he authored. C. E. also made an early impression when "in the early 90's George Case and I published the *Fullerton Journal*." C. E., whose wife was the daughter of John P. Zeyn, one of the original Anaheim settlers, later became very involved in banking before retiring to his residence on East Central Avenue.

This is the home of Herbert "Bert" Ford and Carrie McFadden Ford at the northwest corner of Highland and Commonwealth Avenues, where Fullerton City Hall now stands. Part of the property was later occupied by the offices of Dr. Claude Steen before building of the City Hall in 1962–1963. Photo courtesy of Launer Local History Room, Fullerton Public Library

This photo of George Amerige in a buggy is typical of others taken at various locations in and around the Fullerton townsite in 1887, making for speculation that these were promotional pictures taken in preparation for launching the real estate development which became known as Fullerton. One identification of this particular photo placed the location as what is now downtown Fullerton and the building in the background as the Amerige Brothers Real Estate office which was originally located on South Harbor Boulevard and has been preserved in Amerige Park. Photo courtesy of Launer Local History Room, Fullerton Public Library

Ostriches

Other important pioneers followed in the 1890s, but before leaving the 1880s, we must talk about . . . ostriches.

The Fullerton Ostrich Farm of Edward Atherton located north of Dorothy Lane and east of Acacia Avenue on the property now occupied by Acacia School and St. Juliana's Catholic Church—has been described as the "Knott's Berry Farm of its day"—a prime attraction. Tourists just had to visit the gangly, often ornery, big birds (mature ostriches stood six to eight feet tall and weighed up to four hundred pounds) with the beautiful plumes so desired by the fashion conscious ladies of the day; even the locals liked to visit. "What the boys liked to do best of all was to feed oranges to the big birds. The ostriches liked oranges to eat. They never chewed them. They swallowed the oranges whole. The boys liked to watch the round oranges go GULP, GULP down the long necks of the ostriches!" wrote Dora May Sim in her wonderful book, *Ostrich Eggs For Breakfast (A History of Fullerton For Boys and Girls)*.

It was always quite an adventure, observers of the day have said, to watch the feeding of the ostriches at the Fullerton Ostrich Farm. The ornery birds were known to vent their frustrations with jabs of their beaks and kicks from their powerful legs, and they were prone to turn and run. Yet, as you can see, the feeding was accomplished with regularity. Photo courtesy of Launer Local History Room, Fullerton Public Library

This is the first building on the Fullerton townsite, the real estate office of Edward and George Amerige which, for a time, also served as their home. The office, seen here at its location on the east side of 100 block of North Spadra Road (Harbor Boulevard)— the St. George Hotel can be seen in the background—was originally located on the west side of the 100 block of South Spadra. The restored structure has been preserved in Amerige Park on West Commonwealth Avenue, behind the Senior Citizens Multi-Service Center. Photo courtesy of Launer Local History Room, Fullerton Public Library

All of Fullerton was aware of the ostriches; in the spring you couldn't help it! "In the spring-time, a faraway bellowing coming from the foot-hills of northeast Fullerton would float down into town and children would make their way up through the fields right outside of town . . . and go visit the source of that sound. It was mating season on Ed Atherton's ostrich farm, and the sound of some 200 huge birds singing love songs broke the pastoral stillness and echoed down to the city," Doris Lee wrote in the *Fullerton Daily News-Tribune*.

Blame the phenomenon on Atherton . . . and blame it on the fashionable ladies who simply had to have an ostrich plume to set off their high fashion dress . . . and blame it on economics, for there was a profit to be made in this business.

By August 1886, he had moved 47 birds from Buena Park to their new home on Dorothy Lane and nine chicks were hatched the first year. The innovative Atherton invented an incubator (50 chicks the second year), created a successful marketing plan, and, by 1889, "Fullerton reveled in the title of 'the ostrich capital of the continent' with 127 birds in residence," according to an *Orange Coast Magazine* article in July 1889. But as the century turned, demand for plumes declined and the ostriches began to fade from view. The Atherton farm began to turn out oranges and walnuts, but about a dozen of the big birds remained on display until the mid-twenties when the last of them left Fullerton.

In November 1888, Mr. and Mrs. William Starbuck came to town and opened the first drugstore, the Gem Pharmacy. The Gem had several locations in Fullerton, first on the south side of the 100 block of East Commonwealth Avenue, in the Sansinena Block, and later at locations on Harbor Boulevard. Starbuck played a leading role in getting schools started in Fullerton, being elected as one of the first high school trustees and serving for fifteen years. He was a leader in other ways, too, his store hosting the first "library" and later Fullerton's first telephone company, which he served as manager. Starbuck, after whom the street now known as Valencia Avenue was once named, was a staunch booster of Fullerton, even extending to his Gem Pharmacy stationery which, on its reverse side, carried pictures of Fullerton's and Placentia's beautiful homes and business blocks. William Starbuck, who first lived with his wife in rooms on the second floor of the Chadbourne Building, died at his Highland Avenue home in 1940.

Joining settlers early in the 1890s was J. C. Sheppard, who was born in Arkansas in 1856, came to California in 1875, and to Fullerton in the spring of 1891. He went to work for the Anaheim Union Water Company, becoming superintendent and serving in that capacity for almost nine years before resigning to devote his full attention to his fifty-acre ranch and a cement contracting business. *Pictorial American* said of him in 1909: "Mr. Sheppard is one of the best-known cement contractors in Southern California. He makes a speciality of this work for water systems, and has had contracts of this kind for almost all the prominent water systems in this section of the state." One of his children was Carrie D. Sheppard, who became a Fullerton librarian and wrote several historical pieces now on file in the Launer Local History Room of the Fullerton Public Library.

While the settlers included merchants, most of the early pioneers resided in outlying areas where they made their way by farming, initially providing the necessities to sustain their own lives and then enlarging their operations—as water became available and additional tilling became practical—to where they sold crops for profit. Both Nina Miller's recollections of her grandparents, the Henry Burdorfs, and Mrs. H. C. Babize's story of her parents, the J. B. Stones, said they first grew grains, then grapes, then walnuts and, finally, oranges. The grapes were sold to Anaheim vintners who, in one year in the mid-1880s, produced 800,000 gallons of wine and 187,000 gallons of brandy and liqueurs. Grape production came to an abrupt halt by 1889, however, when grape phyllomera

The "Four Corners" of downtown Fullerton—the intersection of Spadra Road (Harbor Boulevard) and Commonwealth Avenue—as it looked in early 1889. The building at right, at the southeast corner of Spadra and Commonwealth, was built by H. Gaylord Wilshire and was the third built on the townsite. The site is being redeveloped after a New Year's Day fire in 1909 destroyed the original buildings. In the center is the St. George Hotel, "The first significant structure" on the townsite. At left is the Chadbourne Building at the northwest corner of the intersection where Security Pacific Bank was located for many years. Close examination of the center of the picture will reveal a lone gas streetlight at the southwest corner of intersection. The story is told that George Amerige carried the light, a gift of the Anaheim lamplighter, on his shoulder from that city and placed it at this location. Photo courtesy of Launer Local History Room, Fullerton Public Library

disease destroyed the vines and put an end to the wine industry here.

In July 1893, the *Tribune* reported, "—A busy scene to be viewed daily at the Fullerton depot. A constant line of wagons loaded with grain, fruit, potatoes, wool, etc., are arriving from early till late, and inside a number of men are employed in loading cars, weighing, marking and otherwise manipulating the various products of Fullerton's fertile soil." At that writing, orange and lemon production were just starting to take a grip on the local economy. Citrus—producing it, packing it, shipping it—proved, in combination with the railroad, to be the foundation for a flourishing Fullerton.

The Citrus Industry

Citrus was introduced to California in 1769 with arrival of Gov. Gaspar de Portola's expedition to found the missions. The San Gabriel Mission, which held jurisdiction over Fullerton lands, had the most extensive groves in the state, having been set out in 1804 and containing 211 fruit trees by 1818, according to com-

This is a view of the St. George Hotel shortly after it was completed on February 28, 1888. Landscaping has not yet been completed on the 65-room structure which cost $54,000 to build (furnishings cost an additional $15,000). The hotel originally was open only on a "seasonal" basis and also operated under the name of the Hotel Shay. Later, it was home for George Amerige and his bride for many years. The building was razed in 1918, and Amerige constructed the East Commonwealth Avenue and East Amerige Avenue business blocks which remain today. Photo courtesy of Launer Local History Room, Fullerton Public Library

Here is the St. George hotel in all its splendor at about the turn of the century. This photo, with the landscaping having full growth and bicycle and buggy pathways firmly established, was used on picture postcards promoting the hotel and the town. One contention is that the man in the derby hat in the center of the second-floor balcony is George Amerige, after whom the hotel was named. Photo courtesy of Launer Local History Room, Fullerton Public Library

ment by G. W. Sandilands in Samuel Armor's *History of Orange County*, published in 1921.

Fullerton's Charles C. Chapman wrote more about the citrus industry in the Armor history, saying Orange County was the, "ideal section for the culture of the orange . . . the orange grown here has no equal. This is demonstrated by the fact that for years oranges from this county have brought the highest prices, in the most discriminating market of the country, of any oranges grown in the world."

Orange plantings—navels, generally—began extensively in the county in the 1870s. Chapman said R. H. Gilman set trees on his property between Placentia Avenue and State College Boulevard (about the center of the Cal State campus) in 1875 and William McFadden did likewise in 1880, the same year Gilman established the first Valencia orange grove. Growers fought off "black scale" and "red scale" diseases in the late 1870s and 1880s, first with caustic washes, and, later, by fumigating with gas made from cyanide or potassium and sulfuric acid.

Chapman said the first oranges were shipped from the county in 1883 by M. A. Peters and A. D. Bishop, who sent two carloads to Des Moines, Iowa. When the railroad came to Fullerton five years later, the city quickly became a major shipping center, and, attendant to this new status, warehouses and packing houses were developed along the railroad right-of-way. A *Fullerton Tribune* article on January 25, 1896, described the burgeoning industry:

The William Starbuck family came to Fullerton in 1888 from El Modena and opened the Gem Pharmacy, pictured here at its location on the south side of the 100 block of East Commonwealth Avenue. It was demolished when the Odd Fellows built their three-story brick hall in 1927, a structure which now houses the Williams Company. Originally identified as the Schindler-Schumacher-Grimshaw "block," the three buildings shown were identified as the "Sansinena Block" in an 1896 newspaper photo. Photo courtesy of Launer Local History Room, Fullerton Public Library

> *"The shipping from here now has increased to the extent that by actual railroad facts it is show that it far exceeds any other point this side of the southern metropolis. The year 1894 saw 792 carloads of oranges, cabbages, wool, corn, grain and potatoes pass through her different warehouses—seven in number—for near-by points and eastern distribution. It is estimated by our chamber of commerce that this amount will no doubt be doubled when the reckoning is made for 1896."*

A year and a half later—July 3, 1897—the *Tribune* called Fullerton "one of the most important shipping points in Southern California," and reported, "The orange, lemon and walnut industries are prosecuted with vigor and success. . . ." The article went on to note, "Fullerton has three large orange packing houses employing on an average during the orange season, about 75 hands. There are seven various warehouses and all the general business that a town of its size and relative importance in the citrus belt demands. . . . Over 200 carloads of oranges were shipped from this point this season . . . all of which realized good prices, the returns being very satisfactory to the growers. . . . Over $65,000 worth of walnuts were shipped last year. . . . The grain shipments average several hundred carloads every year. . . . The lemons of this section are large and fine and readily find a market everywhere."

In 1899 the *Tribune* reported, "The town maintains its record for being the principal shipping point south of Los Angeles," and Fullerton remained in the

forefront in 1910 when Orange County shipped 840,960 boxes of oranges and 43,392 boxes of lemons. Ten years later—1920—those numbers had climbed to 2,000,000 boxes of oranges and 300,000 boxes of lemons.

The numbers show full well that Fullerton's economics, later sustained by oil production, were founded on the citrus-railroad link. It happened because the region, according to an 1896 *Tribune* story, was blessed with, "a soil that will produce almost anything that is put into it and yield a most bountiful harvest." And, it hap-

William Starbuck is seen here inside the Greater Gem Pharmacy on North Spadra Road. The business also housed Fullerton's first library; the first telephone exchange (the first in Orange County to connect out of town), of which Starbuck was the general manager for twenty-seven years, according to his wife, Flora; and was also, for a time, the site of the post office with Starbuck as postmaster. Starbuck was also a community leader in education, being, with Alexander McDermont, the first to solicit support for a Fullerton Union High School District and serving as a trustee for fifteen years. Photo courtesy of Launer Local History Room, Fullerton Public Library

"Fullerton has one of the most capacious railway stations on the line," said the Fullerton Tribune on August 17, 1895. This photo here shows how it looked soon after it was constructed in 1888. Photo courtesy of Launer Local History Room, Fullerton Public Library

It is now known as Heritage House and rests, lovingly restored, in a beautiful setting in the Fullerton Arboretum on the campus of California State University, Fullerton. But then, in 1895, it was the brand-new home of newlyweds Dr. George C. Clark of Fullerton and his bride, the former Edith Johnston of Norwalk. The home was built by A. D. Porter and H. W. McWilliams for $1,300, just $100 more than the loan Dr. Clark had obtained from the Savings, Loan and Building Association of Anaheim, and was ready for occupancy in early February 1895, slightly more than a month after the December 20, 1894, wedding of the popular couple. Constructed using a lot of redwood as decorative trim with colored glass windows, the house was home and office to Dr. Clark. Tours of the restored Victorian cottage are available. Photo by the author

pened because the town founders convinced the railroad to reroute its line through Fullerton.

Heritage House

A significant 1891 arrival was Dr. George Crook Clark, whose restored home/office, built for his bride in 1894–1895, is on view today at the Fullerton Arboretum on the California State University campus. Dr. Clark was a popular figure in Fullerton and his courting of Edith Johnston was a rather public affair; when he purchased two lots at the corner of Amerige and Harvard (Lemon) it prompted the *Fullerton Tribune* to ask, "What's up, Doc?" The answer became apparent when the doctor got a loan and construction began on the home now called "Heritage house."

But Dr. Clark was much more than the builder of Heritage House. He was not the first doctor in Fullerton—at least one, a Dr. Baker ("he was a tubercular and couldn't practice very much," C. E. Holcomb once recalled) was here before him—but George Clark became its best known. Early on, however, "infamous" might have been a more correct description, at least according to Edgar Johnson, publisher of the *Fullerton Tribune*. The doctor, an avid musician who liked to play his flute for relaxation, had his first offices in the Chadbourne Building, directly above the *Tribune* ("in fact, I slept in my office at the time, too; moved in there and slept there," Dr. Clark once

Fullerton's first school building, a magnificent two-story, four-room brick structure, was constructed at the northeast corner of Wilshire Avenue and Harvard Avenue (Lemon Street) in 1889. Construction was made possible by passage of a $10,000 bond issue in the spring of that year and the students and their parents completed the landscaping—which, it appears was in the works when this photo was taken (probably taken before the first classes opened in the bottom two rooms in the fall of 1889). Photo courtesy of Launer Local History Room, Fullerton Public Library

Faculty and students are seen outside Fullerton's first High School building at the northwest corner of Wilshire and Lawrence avenues. (Lawrence used to run north to Chapman Avenue, which was originally named Northam Avenue). This building housed the high school until it moved to new quarters on Commonwealth Avenue for the start of classes in the fall of 1908, and then was purchased by the elementary school district and used for classrooms. It was torn down in February of 1913 and replaced with a more modern twelve-room facility which was demolished after the 1933 earthquake. The area is now a parking lot. Photo courtesy of Launer Local History Room, Fullerton Public Library

This is the entire student body and faculty of Fullerton Union High School in 1895, two years after the high school district was founded. Pictured are: (top row, from left) W. R. Carpenter, principal (and faculty), Clarence McFadden, Arthur McDermont, Sandy Gardiner, Ralph McFadden, DeWitt Montgomery, Ed Cleaver, and Henry Meiser, Jr.; (middle row, from left) Mabel Porter, Carrie Porter, May Heaslip, Virginia Nicolas, and Cristy Gage; and (front row, from left) Ada Montgomery, Flossie Priest, Lenore Seidel, Frank McDermont, Harry Dunn, and Thomas McFadden. Identifications were reportedly provided by Robert McFadden. Photo courtesy of Launer Local History Room, Fullerton Public Library

The Amerige Brothers Real Estate Office was the first business establishment and first building on the townsite of Fullerton in 1887, and it remained a center of commerce over the next twenty-five to thirty years, even as larger and sturdier structures came on the scene. The building was visited by "cowpokes" and business-suited types when it was located on the east side of the 100 block of North Spadra Road (Harbor Boulevard), seen here probably right after the turn of the century. The preserved, restored building is now located in Amerige Park. Photo courtesy of Launer Local History Room, Fullerton Public Library

said). One day, this statement appeared in the *Tribune:* "Few people stop and think that the newspaper man has many difficulties to contend with. If any of our readers have an idea that they could write a brilliant and brainy editorial in our sanctum, with Dr. Clark with his flute right over head tooting 'Down Went McGinty' to the tune of the 'Dead March,' they are welcome to it."

But all was in jest, and just three years after his arrival the popular Dr. Clark was elected county coroner and public administrator in 1894. He was elected a public school trustee in 1897, re-elected coroner the next year, and, in 1904, was elected one of Fullerton's first city trustees (councilmen). Later, when the city's first Board of Health was formed, Dr. Clark served as its president for ten years. He moved to Los Angeles in 1905, but returned in 1911 and associated with the medical firm of Johnston, Beebe, Clark, Davis and, later, Wickett. Dr. Clark, who died in September 1948, continued in practice until about 1940 and lived his last years in Balboa.

In 1894 another significant pioneer family of East Fullerton made its appearance in the personages of the Orson V. Knowltons who moved to the Acacia-Chapman-Commonwealth area. The Knowltons had five children—Charles, Avis, Kent, Hollis, and Ruth—and several of them have made contributions to historical Fullerton references, including a 1949 report by Charles Knowlton which traces early land ownership in Fullerton. The family, which came to Anaheim from Nebraska in 1886, was very active in Fullerton civic affairs for years in addition to ranch activities on the Fullerton acreage.

Charles C. Chapman

Undoubtedly the best known and influential of Fullerton's "acquisitions" in the 1890s was Charles Clarke Chapman. The Illinois native who, with his brother, Frank, had accumulated a small fortune in publishing, real estate, and other businesses in their native state—before losing a good portion of it in the "bankers' panic" of 1893—made the move west in 1894 for the benefit of his wife's health, going first to her native Texas, but moving on as the summer heat proved too much for her. They settled in Los Angeles, but, sadly, "Even with the best medical attention available, Lizzie's condition rapidly grew worse and on the 23rd of September, 1894, she bade us a final farewell," Chapman wrote in his memoirs. But with the transition from the Midwest made, and, at age forty-one, Chapman and his children, Ethel and C. Stanley, began a new life. It was one which his 1944 obituary in the *Fullerton News-Tribune* said, was, "intimately identified with the development of Southern California."

Following is Charles C. Chapman's account of his purchase of property—extending eastward from what is now State College Boulevard and south from what is now Chapman Avenue—in what was to become East Fullerton:

Charles Clarke Chapman was called "one of the most prominent business men and philanthropists in the southland," when he died at the age of ninety-one at his North Cypress Avenue (State College Boulevard) home in Fullerton on April 5, 1944. Fullerton's first mayor, is, perhaps, best known for the innovative production and marketing methods which established the Valencia orange as a highly viable Southern California industry, prompting the title "Father of the Valencia Orange Industry." He began ranching in Fullerton in 1894 and made this city his home in 1898, built the magnificent family residence on the northeast corner of Cypress (State College) and Commonwealth avenues in 1903, and thereafter achieved virtually unmatched accomplishments in civic leadership. Photo courtesy of Launer Local History Room, Fullerton Public Library

"Shortly after my arrival in Los Angeles, Mr. Rohrer [George Rohrer was a Los Angeles resident who had gone to Chicago to dispose of his heavily encumbered Los Angeles properties], still in Chicago, offered to Frank a fruit ranch in the Placentia area of Orange County in exchange for some of our Chicago property and Frank wired me to inspect this property which Mr. Rohrer's brother would show me. We came to Fullerton on the train and, Mr. Rohrer saying it was only a short distance, I was induced to walk to the ranch. This was really a mistake on his part, since he was desirous of impressing me, as a prospective buyer, with the beauty and value of the property. The walk was long, and I was quite tired when we reached the ranch and I am sure it did not look as attractive as it might have, had I been driven to it and arrived fresh and eager. However, I gave the place a hasty examination and was quite favorably impressed with its possibilities. It was evident that it had been sadly neglected, but I found the soil fertile, the location favorable, and the land all set to fruit trees. I went to the telegraph office at Fullerton and wired Frank a favorable report, and the deal was consummated.

"This ranch property was held in the name of the Placentia Orchard Company and the trade was for the stock of that corporation, which incidentally is among the

The "vast nothingness" that was the townsite of Fullerton in late 1888 is clearly shown in this photograph looking toward the northeast from near the corner of Spadra Road (Harbor Boulevard) and Commonwealth Avenue. The structure on the left is the eastern edge of the St. George Hotel, and at right—with nothing but open land in between—the community's first church, the Presbyterian, is under construction. Photo courtesy of Launer Local History Room, Fullerton Public Library

This is the completed First Presbyterian Church at the southeast corner of Pomona and Wilshire avenues dedicated on June 30, 1889. The church was shared with the Baptists, who later purchased it from the Presbyterians and took sole possession of the property. They outgrew the facility, demolished it, and built their own sanctuary on the same double lot. Photo courtesy of Launer Local History Room, Fullerton Public Library

When the Presbyterians sold to the Baptists, they moved to the northeast corner of Malden and Commonwealth avenues where they constructed this edifice, which Edward R. Amerige called, "the finest church structure in town and a credit to a much larger place than Fullerton." The building, razed in 1955, is seen here in its later years, evidenced by the presence of parking meters on Commonwealth Avenue. Photo courtesy of Launer Local History Room, Fullerton Public Library

oldest in California, having been incorporated in 1892. This beautiful property was named Santa Ysabel Rancho in memory of my dear lost wife."

Charles C. Chapman continued living in Los Angeles, in an elaborate home on a large lot (later home to the Automobile Club of Southern California) even while beginning development of the Fullerton/Placentia property. "My first improvement was a temporary shed to care for my first crop which I had sold to F. P. Fay. Other minor improvements followed. . . , " Charles C. wrote in an autobiography which his son, C. Stanley, had published in his memory. His report on the first year's operations—May 1, 1894 to May 1, 1895—follows:

"Expenditures: Salary $3,131.64; Food $488.60; Blacksmith $46.00; Water $248.44; Fumigating $880.71; Interest $1,927.64; Fertilizing $723.98; Improvement $460.40; Implements $79.00; Incidentals $276.70. Total $8,263.11.
"Receipts: Peach Crop $1,001.45; Walnuts $240.00; Orange $2,439.23; Pumpkins $48.00; Total $3,908.68. Leaving a deficit of $4,354.43."

The second year was worse, Chapman said, because of a mistake he made in spraying the crop with a caustic soda solution . . . but, "I was being educated in this new business and was paying rather heavily for my schooling," so he continued to work the ranch and at the same time was developing business interests in Los Angeles. It was not until after his marriage in Los Angeles to the former Clara Irvin, in September 1898, that the family made the move to Santa Ysabel (where a child, Irvin Clarke Chapman was born to them in February 1911). It was 1899 when Charles C. Chapman arrived to live permanently in Fullerton, initially in a small cottage he had built on the property as a place to stay overnight, but eventually in the showplace, three-story structure at what is now the northeast corner of State College Boulevard and Commonwealth Avenue.

Chapman worked hard at improving his ranch—"I kept on modernizing my operations, putting in improvements as they appeared on the market."—and made a huge success of the citrus business. He acquired more land, the first being 210 acres which extended west ("at varying depths") and north ("about a mile") from the northwest corner of State College and Chapman. It was set to oranges and avocados and Chapman named it Santa Ema [sic] "in honor of my older sister Emma." The ranch was secured in several parcels and at different times from the late 1890s into the 1920s.

Chapman was often referred to as the "Father of the Valencia Orange Industry" because of his innovative growing and marketing methods after noticing that "Valencia lates" were a particularly hardy species that did not fall from the tree, even when over-ripe, and "It, therefore, may be held for the most favorable marketing demands" and was "a splendid keeper . . . therefore a most excellent shipping orange."

But, Charles C. Chapman was not all oranges. Oil production became a prime concern after "Chapman No. 1" gushered in on his Placentia area acreage in 1911; he was a prime mover in real estate development in both Fullerton and Los Angeles; his gifts and guidance as board chairman led to the founding of California Christian College in Los Angeles in 1920, which was renamed in his honor in 1933 and now exists as Chapman University in Orange; he was founding chairman of the board of Bank of America; he was strongly urged to be the vice presidential running mate of Calvin Coolidge in 1924 before he rejected the idea

Methodist Church, Fullerton, Cal.

Fullerton's second church building was constructed by the Methodists in the 100 block of West Amerige Avenue in the early 1890s. They held services in the Grimshaw Building on East Commonwealth Avenue before moving to Chadbourne Hall where they shared space and services with the Presbyterians before building this facility. Photo courtesy of Launer Local History Room, Fullerton Public Library

as he had previously turned down a chance to run for governor of California in 1914; he was the recipient of the "Pioneer Preeminent Medal" from the YMCA; he established Nantungchow Hospital in China in 1906; and he was Fullerton's first mayor in 1904.

Charles C. Chapman's role among those foremost in leading Fullerton into the next century is unquestioned, and his name will appear prominently in this continuing chronology. But there were others, as C. E. Holcomb said:

"Who really made Fullerton a decent place in which to live? It was not the saloons, poker joints and so-called billiard parlors and those who ran them in the early days . . . It was people and families like the McDermonts, Daniels, Schultz's, Sheppards, Spragues, Evans, Carltons, Gardiners, Starbucks, Vails and others like them who started the churches and Sunday schools and kept them going no matter how tough and difficult the way—'and their works do follow them.'"

P. A. Schumacher operated Orange County Real Estate, one of Fullerton's first, and also built one of the first buildings on the south side of the 100 block of East Commonwealth Avenue. This was his home at the northeast corner of Richman and Commonwealth avenues as it appeared in 1894. Photo courtesy of Launer Local History Room, Fullerton Public Library

Dr. George C. Clark, who came to Fullerton in 1891, was not the city's first physician, but he is well remembered for his medical achievements as well as for having built the home/office which stands today in the Cal State Fullerton Arboretum and is known as "Heritage House." In 1894, Dr. Clark was elected Orange County coroner, and he later was a member of Fullerton's first Board of Trustees (City Council) in 1904, was a school trustee and served as president of the city Board of Health. He and his family moved to Los Angeles in 1905, but returned to Fullerton in 1911 where they lived for many years before moving to their beach home on Balboa Island. He practiced medicine until about 1940 and died of heart disease in 1948 at the age of eighty-five. Photo courtesy of Launer Local History Room, Fullerton Public Library

The flatlands of the Botsford Ranch in East Fullerton are apparent in this photo of seedlings being placed on the property. The old Botsford Ranch House and winery (to the right of it) are visible in the background of this picture, apparently a view to the southeast, which has been dated 1891 in Fullerton Public Library files. Close inspection of the figure in the foreground could lead one to believe it is William L. Hale. Photo courtesy of Launer Local History Room, Fullerton Public Library

Indeed, the churches, schools, library and businesses that built Fullerton, the institutions which we, to this day, hold most dear, were created during this era by the pioneers we have discussed. Before departing this period, we will review them, including the story of how Orange County came to be and Fullerton's role in it.

Fullerton Schools

Creation of the Fullerton School District, taking in parts of the Orangethorpe, Placentia, and Anaheim districts, all then in Los Angeles County, occurred in 1888. An initial two-week session of classes was held during the summer, to get an idea of full class enrollment starting in September of that year, the setting being an abandoned blacksmith shop at Santa Fe and Pomona avenues, where Edwin Clark was the first teacher. A highlight, according to Grace McDermont Ford, a member of that first class, was the visit of a gopher snake from under one of the benches nailed to the shop wall: "From that time on, the girls all sat in oriental fashion: (with their legs crossed under them on the bench)." Perhaps because of the snake and other discomforts in the dirt-floored building, classes for the regular school session in September were moved to the second floor of the Sansinena Building on East Commonwealth. Average daily attendance that first school year was about forty pupils.

In the spring of 1889, a bond issue of $10,000—"People just threw up their hands and said that we wouldn't need that large a school building for fifty years."—was passed and Fullerton's first public school building was constructed, a two-story, four-room brick building at the northeast corner of Lemon Street and Wilshire Avenue. The pupils did a lot of the landscaping themselves and classes opened there—in the two rooms on the lower floor only, the faculty having been doubled . . . to two teachers—in the fall of that same year. At the end of that school year, in 1890, Grace McDermont (Ford) was the first graduating class—the lone member. In the fall of 1891, Mr. R. Pendleton took charge of the school and in 1892 a third teacher was added. Fullerton public education was underway.

High School

"In the summer of 1892 William Starbuck and Alex. McDermont canvassed the northern part of Orange County, hoping to transform educational ideas into action," Louis Plummer wrote in his book, *Fullerton Union High School and Junior College 1893–1943*. In the spring of 1893 a petition subscribed to by 29 electors of the Placentia School District, 107 of the Fullerton District, 15 of the

Orangethorpe, and 18 of Buena Park, was sent to the Orange County superintendent of schools:

> "We the undersigned Trustees and electors of the School Districts of Placentia, Fullerton, Orangethorpe and Buena Park, this County and State, do hereby petition that you do call an election in above named districts in accordance with assembly bill No. 57 of the Assembly of this State, for the purpose of establishing a high school for said precincts."

County Schools Superintendent J. P. Greeley issued a notice of election on April 18, 1893; an election was held on April 29, 1893, and the vote overwhelmingly favored formation of the district—but it didn't happen. It seems that election boards in some districts failed to make an appearance and some electors were unable to cast ballots. The district attorney ruled another vote must be held; it was, at the end of May, and the Fullerton Union High School District was created with only eight dissenting votes. The *Fullerton Tribune* said:

> "The high school election is now over again. This time the district attorney has decided it is 'a go.' We never felt better in our lives; Thank you! . . . A. McDermont and J. A. Vail deserve much credit for hard work with men and teams to see that every man had a way of getting to the polls here. Orangethorpe went solid for it, Placentia was two-thirds for it and all the votes cast in Buena Park were for it . . . ."

William Starbuck, A. S. Bradford (secretary), B. F. Porter and Dr. D. W. Hasson, and Henry Schultz (president) were the first trustees, W. R. Carpenter was selected the first principal (and sole faculty) at a salary of $125 a month (later reduced to $115) and classes began with eight students in rented quarters on the second floor of the grammar school at Lemon Street and Wilshire Avenue. The first graduating class in 1896 consisted of Thomas McFadden and Arthur Staley. Brea and La Habra and then Richfield, Commonwealth, Yorba, and Yorba Linda school districts joined the original Fullerton, Buena Park, Orangethorpe, and Placentia districts and, soon after the start of classes in the fall of 1898, the high school moved into its own building, a brand new structure at the northwest corner of Lawrence and Wilshire avenues that, "would be a credit to a city of 10,000 inhabitants." It would be "home" until after the turn of the century.

Library
A single shelf of books in the Gem Pharmacy in 1888 marked the start of Fullerton's Public Library—albeit a rather informal one. Mr. and Mrs. William Starbuck made those books available to anyone interested in reading them, and the tradition was established. It was carried on at the turn of the century by Mrs. James Dean, wife of a pioneer dentist, who set up a free reading room on the second floor of the Chadbourne Building with the admitted purpose of providing "young men with a wholesome alternative to the town saloons." After the Deans left the city, the reading room continued under the direction of a committee of interested citizens until advent of the first organized library system after the Library Board of Trustees was established in 1906.

Newspapers
Fullerton's first newspaper was called the *New Era*, according to George

Edgar Johnson, seen here in 1898 at his desk in his Fullerton office, brought newspapering to Fullerton to stay and played an influential role in building the townsite from its infancy until selling the Fullerton Daily News-Tribune *in 1929. His weekly grew with the town and he converted it to a daily newspaper in 1914, purchased the* Fullerton News *in 1926 and merged the two papers into the* Fullerton News-Tribune, *a name which remains today. Though the feisty editor's feuds with some of the town's leading citizens are well documented, most of the squabbles were patched up over the years and Johnson's contributions to Fullerton's growth have been recognized. He died on May 16, 1935, at about the age of sixty-seven. Photo courtesy of Launer Local History Room, Fullerton Public Library*

William L. Hale was a mayor of Fullerton (two terms says he, three terms says the city record) whose East Chapman Avenue winery and residence (now the Montessori Child Development Center) were local landmarks. The Vermont native came to Fullerton—which he called "the greatest place on earth"—in 1886, began work on the W. F. Botsford ranch in 1887, and purchased the property in 1889. The popular boxer (he once knocked out a man who "came out from Chicago to give me a whipping" in an abbreviated contest on the steps of the Hotel Shay), race horse breeder and auto racer (he beat Barney Oldfield at Ascot Park), also served as an Orange County sheriff, as president of the high school Board of Trustees, vice president of First National Bank, organizing director and president of Fullerton Savings and Loan Association, twenty-year Masonic board president, and Placentia Orange Growers Association president. In a memoir, he admitted to making mistakes about two investment opportunities, the first being a pre-1890 opportunity to purchase—"for one dollar an acre"—the Brea hills land where he was grazing sheep. "I was not interested, as oil was coming out of the ground and no grass would grow. As I look back, what a terrible mistake I made." Then, there was the time Henry Ford, "wanted me to invest in some of the stock in his company. The offer was 1,000 shares at 10 cents a share." Hale called his rejection of the offer a "foolish mistake." Photo courtesy of Launer Local History Room, Fullerton Public Library

Amerige, who reports he held an interest in it and was instrumental in moving it from Anaheim to Fullerton in 1888. Historian Jim Sleeper, in *Turn the Rascals Out!*, said the weekly *New Era* commenced publication in May 1887 and died in September 1889. George A. Field was the editor. Then, there was the *Fullerton Star* published by Winfield Clarke Hogaboom, which, Sleeper said, "first shone on April 26, 1889, and went out in September of the same year." Sleeper also tells us about the *Fullerton Journal*, initiated in January 1891 by C. E. (Chet) Holcomb and George Case, who sold it to Jim Nugent, who moved it to Anaheim in 1892. Later that year it went "where the woodbine twineth," Sleeper quoted the *Santa Ana Standard* as reporting. In 1902 the *Fullerton News* made its appearance, with Vivian Tresslar (later to become postmaster) listed as "editor and proprietor." However, in his autobiography, Charles Chapman says it was he who "bought complete modern equipment for a small printing plant and secured Vivian Tresslar as editor. On January 3, 1902, there appeared the first issue of the *Fullerton News*." The *News* lived long enough to become a daily paper before being absorbed by the newspaper which has survived through the years to this date, the *Fullerton Tribune*.

Edgar Johnson started his *Tribune* in Westminster in 1890 and began publishing in Fullerton, at the behest of George Amerige and Alex McDermont, on April 1, 1893—a date which has been the subject of considerable debate. Some have claimed the paper was established in 1891—the words "Established in 1891" for years boldly arched over the office doors at 120 West Wilshire Avenue—and this writer admits to perpetuating that date in previous writings. Sleeper says he leaves the *Tribune*'s "bewildering chronology . . . to more patient scholars to untangle," but adds in page notes that, "It is believed that 1893 is likelier (the correct date)." Support for that argument is found in what could be considered "from the horses mouth" evidence in the *Fullerton Tribune* edition of April 3, 1897 (page 3, column 4) where, under the headline, "SINCE APRIL 1ST, 1893," there appears these words (presumably penned by Johnson):

"The Tribune *made its appearance in Fullerton just four years ago . . . Attempts have been made several times to establish a successful local paper here, but none of the promotors succeeded. The editor did not ask anyone to give him a dollar, but only requested a guarantee of 300 subscribers to begin with. Twenty enterprising citizens raised the required amount of cash to pay for the 300 subscriptions, and with the exception of a few dollars, the whole amount was paid in . . . Stern and Goodman had the largest ad in the first issue of the* Tribune *. . . The business of the firm is now probably double what it was in April, 1893."*

The *Tribune* became a daily in January 1914; "absorbed" the *News* in February 1926, (becoming the *News-Tribune*); then became a weekly again in January, 1985. It is published today as the *Fullerton News-Tribune*.

Other Businesses

While the Amerige Real Estate office was the first business in town, two others of particular note followed close behind, both in the same building and both founded in this era. The first is the Ford and Howell grocery store, also site of Fullerton's first post office; the second is the Stern and Goodman general merchandise store, which rapidly grew to become Fullerton's best known "conglomerate" and dealt in all sorts of goods as well as real estate and other activities out of its Fullerton headquarters and several branch stores. Carrie McFadden Ford has related for us the story of her husband's store and Fullerton's first post office:

This photo was taken on the occasion of William L. Hale's marriage in 1906 to the former Joan Ellen Nichols. The happy couple are at the left and the man at the right is unidentified in this photo apparently taken at the Orange County Courthouse. Hale was first married to Dora Bosche in 1893 and two sons, Lee and Harold, were born before her death in 1898. Two daughters—Blanche and Gelene—were born to the second marriage. This photo was a gift to the Fullerton Public Library by a grandson of William Hale. Photo courtesy of Launer Local History Room, Fullerton Public Library

The large brick winery owned by William L. Hale was located on the north side of East Chapman Avenue and at one time was surrounded by one of the largest vineyards in the state. In a Sketch of My Life, *Hale said the vineyard was in place when he purchased the property from W. F. Botsford in 1889, but the grapes later "developed a blight and killed off my entire vineyard." Hale tells this story about the demise of the winery: "I had a number of men working for me in the winery. I had to fire one because of noncooperation. It made him real mad. He returned on the night of July 9 [1897], set fire to the winery and burned it to the ground. I lost all my equipment as well as 8 race horses I had raised." Hale used brick from the winery to build his home at 2025 East Chapman Avenue, which now hosts the Montessori Child Development Center. Photo courtesy of Launer Local History Room, Fullerton Public Library*

The Pictorial American and Town Talk *of April 1909 called it a home "that any man, be he pauper or millionaire, might envy." The* William L. Hale *residence was constructed in 1907–1908. Hale wrote, "I removed the bricks from the burned out winery and used them to build the two-story, tile-roofed house where I now live." The* Pictorial American *of 1909 reported, "The walls are of the best brick with an outside covering of cement and it has a genuine red tile roof. The walls of the house are painted but the combination is charming and the whole presents a most attractive ensemble. The house contains ten rooms and a bath and are all perfectly appointed and elegantly furnished in every detail." The residence, at 2025 East Chapman Avenue, today hosts the Montessori Child Development Center, which has made extensive additions to the property. Photo courtesy of Launer Local History Room, Fullerton Public Library*

"In the fall of '87 Mr. Ford . . . decided to go to Los Angeles and go into the photography business, as he had been a photographer before he came to California. His brother-in-law (Howell) and sister's family had just come to California. Telling them of the new town that was starting in Orange County they decided to come down and look over the ground to start a store. They liked the outlook, rented the south store in the Wilshire Building (southeast corner of Harbor and Commonwealth), laid in a stock of goods, groceries, hardware, crockery and feed, and moved into the building in January of '88 before the building was quite completed. They had a delivery wagon and soon had a fine trade. In the north store room was a furniture [dealer] and undertaker. As too few new people came in and nobody died, he [furniture dealer/undertaker] moved away within a year."

Soon after she married Herbert Ford in May 1889, Ford bought Howell out. Ford applied to the government for a post office in the store, an application which was granted, but "Because he [Ford] was a Republican in a Democratic Administration he was not appointed postmaster. So Mr. [Ed] Beazley [a store employee] was appointed the first postmaster. The office was in the store," Mrs. Ford recalled.

In the winter of 1889, Ford became ill with a severe cold "which turned into pneumonia, from which he never fully recovered." He sold the store in 1890 and the post office was moved to Starbuck's Gem Pharmacy, with William Starbuck becoming postmaster. In October, 1894, after returning from a camping trip with his parents and working all day with a helper on his peach crop, Mrs. Ford said her husband, "took another bad cold and passed away in three days."

Stern and Goodman had assumed the corner location of the furniture dealer and undertaker. It was the start of something big. From this humble beginning grew an enterprise which, by 1909, occupied an enlarged building (two hundred feet of frontage and eighty feet of depth) with fifteen internal departments. Historian Esther Cramer makes several references to the store in her book, *La Habra: The Pass Through The Hills*, including this vivid description of its operations:

"The most active merchants in the local area during the settlement period and on past . . . were Stern and Goodman of Fullerton. Advertising that they handled everything from a needle to a threshing machine, this company had regular delivery routes which served the needs of the ranchers farthest from town.

"The deliveryman served as a lifeline between civilization and rural living for many pioneers. Delivery of supplies brought world news as well as weather reports, vital statistics and local gossip. Orders were placed for the next delivery at each visit, so there was a continuous exchange of information along with the provisions.

"The Stern and Goodman man also was a trader, dealing in butter, eggs, and other produce available from the ranches. Some settlers also handled the sale of

their crops through this diversified business and kept an annual account at Stern and Goodman's. Harvest time meant time for settlement of the year's bills.

"So huge were the operations of Stern and Goodman, they amassed large fortunes. Much capital was reinvested in land, and their 'Sterns Realty Company' became one of the largest landholders in Orange County, besides handling real estate transactions for clients. Much of the land . . . subdivided in 1909 to become Yorba Linda had been included in Stern's holdings."

The "Stern" half of Stern and Goodman was Jacob Stern, who was born in Saxony in 1859, came to America in 1884, and worked in Cleveland, Ohio, for five years before coming to Fullerton and forming a partnership with Joseph Goodman. He married Sarah Laventhal in 1891 and the couple settled in Fullerton, Mrs. Stern's "native city," according to J. M. Guinn in his 1907 book, *A History of California.* They moved to Hollywood in 1904 (corner of Prospect and Vine), but Stern remained a full partner in the Fullerton-based business which his younger brother, August "Gus" Stern, managed for many years after coming to Fullerton in 1899 via San Francisco and Los Angeles. All the while the holdings of the Stern Realty Company continued to grow, prompting Guinn to conclude his Stern biography with: "Starting out in this new world a total stranger and with little means, what Mr. Stern has accomplished   is little short of marvelous and displays the quality of his mettle as no mere words can."

Joseph Goodman was a native of Germany, born in December 1864, who came to America at the age of nineteen. He was just twenty-four when he partnered with Jacob Stern in the Fullerton enterprise. When the pair incorporated into two companies in 1911, Goodman became president of Stern and Goodman Mercantile Company, running the main Fullerton store and its branches in Anaheim, Olive, and Placentia, and vice-president of Stern Realty Company. (Stern took over presidency of the later and vice-presidency of the former). Goodman died in Los Angeles in 1912, three months shy of his forty-eighth birthday.

Fred Strauss, who came to Fullerton from New York to work for Jacob Stern

This photo shows workers in the citrus fields of Fullerton. The scene has been identified as coming from the Klokee Ranch, the location of which is not precisely known. An interesting aspect of the picture is that many of the field workers appear to be Chinese. Hale recalled hiring Chinese labor to build roads in the Ontario area in 1885. Photo courtesy of Launer Local History Room, Fullerton Public Library

These pictures show workers in and around Fullerton packing houses in the 1890s period. The first picture was donated to the Fullerton Public Library by Grace McDermont Ford and shows workers and a wagon outside the "Orange Growers Warehouse." The second scene, reportedly taken in 1889–1900, is of male and female workers inside an unidentified Fullerton packing house. Photos courtesy of Launer Local History Room, Fullerton Public Library

in 1909 (for $18 per week)—and later, with his cousin, Felix Stein, became an owner of Stein and Strauss men's clothing store which occupied the former Stern and Goodman quarters—talked extensively in June 1976, with California State University, Fullerton, Oral History Program interviewer Esther Katz about the Stern and Goodman operation. His observations included these about the company's financial policies:

"In those days, we had very little cash business; it was all on credit. I believe, in those days, people were a little bit more honest than they are today. . . . The farmers used to come in from all over the country, clear from El Toro, to buy two or three hundred dollars worth of merchandise. We gave them credit for a solid year. Then they would come back at the end of the year, when their crop came in, and pay us off; then we used to pay off our creditors. Also, the people would come in with eggs, butter and so forth; and we gave them credit for the groceries they bought . . . we never lost any money, just a few dollars."

First Bank

With commerce growing, it was inevitable that the town would need a bank and it came about in September 1895, with opening of the Fruit Growers Bank (a name selected over The Bank of Fullerton and Walnut Growers' Bank, among other suggestions). On June 8, 1895, the *Fullerton Tribune* announced, "Fullerton is to have a banking institution. This is indicative of the healthy development that the country tributary to Fullerton is enjoying. Banks only go where there is business in hand, and the well supported promise of more to come."

On July 6, the *Tribune* announced the bank had been organized. Directors included W. B. Wilshire, Jacob Stern, Alexander McDermont, H. Gaylord Wilshire, L. C. McKnight, R. G. Balcom, Paul Seeger, Erwin Barr, and J. F. Davis, with Balcom elected president, Seeger vice-president, and Edward R. Amerige, secretary. Edward R. Amerige, Jacob Stern, J. C. Sheppard, M. H. Dunn, Alexander McDermont, A. Barrows, F. R. Holcomb, J. F. Davis, William Starbuck, Charles Binder, William Schulte, Henry Meiser, R. Means, J. H. Clever, and S. F. Daniels were the Fullerton shareholders listed. The bank opened in the "bank room" of the Chadbourne Building on September 3, 1895 and a total of $6,200 was deposited the first day, marking the bank as "A Solid Banking Institution," according to the *Tribune*.

Charles Clarke Chapman said this three-story home at the northeast corner of Cypress (State College) and Commonwealth "was built for comfortable living, not as a 'show piece.' It was, however, probably the most commodious home in Orange County." A series of housewarmings were held by the Chapmans, welcoming friends from throughout the Southland, among them the hosting of Fullerton's very first Board of Trustees (City Council) soon after the successful incorporation election of 1904. C. C. Chapman described the home, seen here in a front view looking toward the east, like this: "The house contained a large living room, a comfortable library with black marble fireplace, a breakfast room, and seven bedrooms on the second floor with two more on the third floor. Much of the third floor was devoted to a large hall, most frequently used by the children and grandchildren as a playroom." Photo courtesy of Launer Local History Room, Fullerton Public Library

Chamber of Commerce

And where there is commerce, you will usually find a Chamber of Commerce. On May 25, 1895, the *Tribune* announced that such an organization had been organized the previous Saturday. "Nearly all of our business men were present, and a number of farmers and fruit growers were in attendance," at the meeting where Alexander McDermont presided as chairman. Directors elected were L. B. Benchley, Jacob Stern, Edward R. Amerige, Benjamin Franklin Porter, and William McFadden, despite the latter's remarks that "one chamber of commerce—the one recently organized at Anaheim—was enough for the northern part of the county." McFadden resigned his post at the group's first meeting the following week and George B. Key was elected to fill his spot at a meeting the week after that. The group's By-Laws established dues at "50 cents per month, payable monthly in advance, or $5.00 per year, if paid annually in advance . . ." and clearly stated the group's purpose:

"The object of this organization shall be to foster and encourage commerce; to stimulate home trade; manufactories; to assist in securing a market for home products; to induce immigration; to assist in the development of the vast resources of Fullerton and surrounding country; to keep our streets and sidewalks clean and in good condition; to advertise this section of Orange county; and to improve our town in every way possible."

Orange County

Two years after the Fullerton townsite map was officially filed with the County of Los Angeles, the community had a new "parent," becoming part of a brand new county—even though this community's electors were decidedly negative about the proposal.

Orange County—source of the name has been debated by historians, but Jim Sleeper has traced it back to an 1871 county proposal when the name was selected to suggest the mediterranean nature of this area's climate and thereby encourage immigration (oranges as a revenue crop were then only a twinkling in

This pre-1940s photo is of the Placentia Orange Growers Association packing house on Commonwealth Avenue at Lawrence Avenue. Warehouses, seven of them in the 1890s, and packing houses, at least three of them in that period, operated in the area north and south of the railroad. For two or three years in the early 1890s another important business operation in the rapidly growing railroad shipping community was a cannery operated by the Joycelyn Brothers in a two-story wooden building at the southeast corner of Malden and Santa Fe avenues. Photo courtesy of Launer Local History Room, Fullerton Public Library

some ranchers' eyes)—had tried to emerge as early as 1870 when Maximilian Stroebel proposed that all territory south of the San Gabriel River separate from Los Angeles. In all, five attempts at division from Los Angeles were made before the effort was successful in 1889.

The governor appointed a commission of five men—including William McFadden of Placentia—to perfect organization of the county and the commissioners called for an election on June 4, a two-thirds majority being needed to confirm creation of the new county. The official canvass of ballots on June 10 showed 2,509 in favor of the county and 500 against

Women took over the work force in Fullerton's packing houses as this photo from the collection of O. M. Thompson attests. Lemons are being packed here under the labels of A 1 of the American Fruit Company and Sun Class Brand. Photo courtesy of Launer Local History Room, Fullerton Public Library

it, and Orange County—with a population of 13,589 and three (Santa Ana, Anaheim, Orange) incorporated cities—was created by a 5-1 plurality. Interestingly, in Fullerton—where voting was held at the Amerige Brothers Real Estate office with J. B. McCullough, Alexander Gardiner, Edward R. Amerige, John Evans, J. P. Greeley and H. G. Wilshire as election officials—the vote was 15 in favor and 96 opposed to creation of the new county (whose name, historian Sleeper has noted, rhymes with no other word in the dictionary).

In a second election on July 17, Santa Ana was selected as the county seat and the first supervisors were elected—William H. Spurgeon, Jacob Ross, Sheldon Littlefield, Samuel Armor, and A. Guy Smith—were elected. (Eugene E. Edwards was elected district attorney and Greeley, of the Fullerton Election Board, was elected county superintendent of schools. The Orange County Board of Supervisors met for the first time on August 5, 1889.

Thus, as we head into a new century, a new town—Fullerton—and a new county—Orange—have been forever emblazoned upon the maps of Southern California. Both have already started the phenomenal growth that would characterize their existence for the next seventy years.

This photo of the W. A. Connoly blacksmith shop from Fullerton Public Library files indicates it was taken in 1890. Notations on the back of the original photo said this shop also belonged at one time to John Gardiner, a member of Fullerton's first City Council. Photo courtesy of Launer Local History Room, Fullerton Public Library

Charles C. Chapman may have been most famous for his Valencia oranges—and his oil wells, and his real estate developments—but the Chapman ranch properties were also well known for their walnut production. Here two wagon loads of "Old Mission Brand"—the famous Chapman trademark brand—are being hauled to the warehouse to await shipment to the lucrative eastern market. Photo courtesy of Launer Local History Room, Fullerton Public Library

The 100 block of South Spadra Road (Harbor Boulevard) in Fullerton was a popular gathering place in the years before the turn of the century. Alex Henderson's blacksmith shop on the west side of the street, about in the middle of the block, was one of the reasons and the building itself had a place in history. C. E. Holcomb and others report that this building was the first blacksmith shop in Fullerton, initially located on the east side of Pomona Avenue (behind the present Post Office building) where, according to Holcomb, "It was operated by two Negroes." Holcomb, who came to Fullerton with his family in 1888, said he, "took work to them when it was necessary and they were good workmen." Otto Stroebel, nephew of the more famous Max Stroebel of Anaheim, and Harry Savage were the next owners and operated the business on the same site. They sold the place to Alex Henderson who moved it to Spadra. The building at left, advertising a barber ship and baths, later became well known as a pool hall. Photo courtesy of Launer Local History Room, Fullerton Public Library

This is the "business end" of the Alex Henderson blacksmith shop in the 100 block of South Spadra Road (Harbor Boulevard). Here, the smithies worked over the hot forge, hammering horseshoes into the proper shape and shoeing horses. They also built carriage and wagon parts and did carriage painting (note the sign) on the premises. Photo courtesy of Launer Local History Room, Fullerton Public Library

Jim Gardiner's Eureka Stables are seen in this photo taken near the turn of the century. Gardiner, also a deputy constable died from pneumonia after rescuing people from flood waters on New Years Day in 1900. Photo courtesy of Launer Local History Room, Fullerton Public Library

South Spadra Road (Harbor Boulevard) at the turn of the century boasted full blocks of buildings on both sides of the street. This photo shows Fullerton's first car, a homemade model owned by John Hiltscher, putting down the middle of the road and drawing the attention of passersby. The two-story brick Fullerton Hotel owned by Mrs. Dierksen (left) was at the northwest corner of Spadra and Santa Fe and north of it on the west side of Spadra was the pool hall and then Alex Henderson's blacksmith shop. Photo courtesy of Launer Local History Room, Fullerton Public Library

CHAPTER VII

A City Takes Shape

1900–1920

It was not a pleasant start to the new century for Fullerton, as disaster, in the form of flood water, visited itself upon the still fledgling community. New Year's Day, 1900, found much of the downtown under eight to twelve inches of water and mud and the incident turned tragic when it claimed the life of one of the town's prominent citizens, blacksmith James Gardiner.

Charles Knowlton explains in a 1949 history that the course of Brea Creek had been changed to run westerly rather than its natural southeasterly route and, in the fall of 1899, a crew had cleared the creek banks of a choking cane break planted years before to prevent erosion. Two solid days of rain closed out 1899 and flood waters pushed the felled cane against a low bridge, effectively damming the westward flow. "This caused the water to overflow the creek banks and inundate most of the business section of Fullerton on New Year's Day," Knowlton said. John R. Gardiner, in a 1955 interview, said his brother, a deputy constable, had gone to the rescue of two young girls stranded by the flood in the north part of town. James "immediately swam his horse across the creek to rescue them. By the time he got them to safety he was exhausted and dropped off to sleep without changing to dry clothes. He took sick with pneumonia and was dead four days later."

Incorporation

As the city recovered from that disaster, serious discussion began on the matter of incorporation. "The new railway was a midwife and John Barleycorn watched through a window when people cast their ballots approving incorporation of the city of Fullerton," was how Fullerton's emergence as a city was described by one periodical in January of 1904. It was a neat summary of what had transpired virtually since the townsite's inception, i.e., debate on the benefits and disadvantages of incorporation with the matter of saloons central to any such discussion.

At the turn of the century the townsite of Fullerton "boasted" four saloons, well supported by those who favored them and looked upon with disdain by many community leaders. "I have always been opposed to liquor in any form, and especially the public saloon . . . a system I believed would debauch our men and

There was more than just football and base-ball on the sports scene at Fullerton Union High School, the proof being found in this picture of Girls Basketball Team of 1910–1911. Team members have been identified on the back of an original photo as, standing, from left, Marie des Granges, Ruth Loughboro, and Gladys Conley, and, below, from left, Helen Horner, Helen Johnson, and Madeline Sherwood. Photo courtesy of Launer Local History Room, Fullerton Public Library

This bird's-eye view of Fullerton was apparently taken looking South in the early 1900s. It would appear that the street running from left to right across the photo, near the center, is West Wilshire Avenue because what seems to be the rear to the Methodist Church in the 100 block of West Amerige Avenue can be seen beyond it at the right/center of the picture. The brick building to the left of the church, at center/left, could be the Masonic Building (Book Harbor). Photo courtesy of Launer Local History Room, Fullerton Public Library

boys and cause prospective residents to turn from us . . ." was Charles C. Chapman's clearly stated opinion on the subject. Others, however, cited not only their individual and constitutional rights but claimed any new city would need the revenue from saloon licenses in order to sustain itself.

As early as 1901 the issue was put to the test. At the end of September, a vote on incorporation was held; the result was 55 votes favoring cityhood and 101 against it. The *Tribune*'s Edgar Johnson favored incorporation, and somewhat reluctantly bowed to the will of the people, writing on September 28, 1901:

"Many of us believed the welfare of the town would be advanced by incorporation, but a large majority of citizens who were equally honest in their convictions thought otherwise, and we should respect their judgment as we would have them respect ours if we were the victors."

The editor issued a call for unity, and properly predicted the results of a future attempt at incorporation:

"It is possible for us to do much toward the upbuilding of the town without a city government and if every citizen will do his part the time is not far distant when incorporation will come as a natural consequence of growth in population and commercial importance, and practically without a contest.

"Everyone who owns a foot of soil can contribute to the general advancement of the whole community by enhancing the beauty of his own holdings, and the reward for his labor is abundant and certain in the shape of increased value, in addition to the enjoyment of a pleasant home.

"Let us work together for the general good of all."

Johnson, that same day, also made it clear he did not like the tactics or the words of the opposition, citing especially a "scurrelous circular" distributed by E. K. Benchley which "impugned the motives of the editor of the *Tribune*." However, a short time later Benchley and Johnson worked together on projects for the mutual advancement of Fullerton.

Two-plus years later, voters were again invited to the pools, this time to ballot on an enlarged area of incorporation encompassing eighteen square miles. A barrage of editorial comment preceded the election, all favoring the idea and this time, some anti-saloon people were on the side of incorporation, including

Benchley and Charles Chapman. When supervisors granted the petition the "large delegation of Fullertonites returned home in Gardiner's tally-ho and buggies, all blowing horns and rejoicing over the decision of the board."

A *Tribune* editorial January 14, 1904, headlined "Incorporation Assured," was right about the election's outcome, despite opponents' claims that incorporation was "tantamount to having a saloon on every corner and houses of ill-repute in between" and opposition from some outlying ranchers concerned that townsite residents would run the whole show.

"VOTERS FAVOR CITY" said the *Tribune* headline, announcing, "The vote on the question of incorporation was 185 yeas to 44 noes," and telling readers:

"Incorporation has carried. Fullerton is to become a city of the sixth class and another step will be made in the upbuilding of an energetic, thriving community. The decision of the voters is to be commended, and the big majority with which they accompanied it shows that their sterling good sense controlled their judgment on election day. The future will approve their wisdom."

Fullerton's first trustees (councilmen) were (with votes in parentheses): John R. Gardiner (143), Edward R. Amerige (136), Dr. George C. Clark (132), E. K. Benchley (129) and Charles C. Chapman (125). This group included a state assemblyman (Amerige) and a native of what was now Fullerton (Gardiner). Other officers elected were W. A. Barnes, city marshal; George Ruddock, city clerk; and J. E. Ford, city treasurer. At the council's first meeting, held in city

The Hiltscher Brothers, John and August, ran the young Fullerton community's most popular meat market—Center Meats. Their delivery wagon is seen in this picture. August Hiltscher served on the Fullerton City Council from 1908 to 1912 and again from 1913 to 1918 and Hiltscher Park in Fullerton is named in his honor. His son, Herman, later was Fullerton city engineer and became the city's first city administrator. John Hiltscher was said to have the first car in town. Photo courtesy of Launer Local History Room, Fullerton Public Library

"Fullerton-Placentia District leads the world in Valencia Oranges and is the largest shipping point in Orange Co." is boldly proclaimed on "Fullerton Exhibit No. 2." Everything from pumpkins to squash, watermelons, oranges, lemons, walnuts, and other goods are displayed on the wagon attended by two unidentified men in their Sunday best. Photo courtesy of Launer History Room, Fullerton Public Library

attorney Emerson J. Marks' office, trustees elected Chapman mayor (after he initially declined Amerige's nomination), selected a city seal (the state coat of arms surrounded by the words *City of Fullerton of California*), called an election on officers for April 11 as required by state law, and initiated discussion on salaries, fees, and proposed ordinances. Regarding the latter, trustees decided to rename Northam Avenue to Chapman Avenue, slated a vote on the liquor license issue, and made it unlawful, among other things, to: fight or brawl, except in necessary self-defense; assault, beat, wound or bruise any other person or persons, or to whoop, halloo, yell or in any way disturb the peace; drive or ride any animal or vehicle through any street in a furious manner, or at a rate of speed to exceed eight miles an hour; have pig pens within two hundred feet of a residence; cut down any trees or shrubs, or dig up any soil without permission of trustees; have any female clothe herself in male attire, or any male clothe himself in female attire, and travel about or appear on the public streets; and, for any vagrant to be within the city limits without visible means of support. It was made clear: "all idle and dissolute persons, all women of ill-repute, and all common drunkards shall be deemed vagrants."

In April, residents voted 158 to 133 to grant saloon licenses and the original Board of Trustees and officers again won approval. The liquor license issue was settled temporarily, but Chapman made clear "it was not only against my principles to sign saloon licenses, which as Mayor I was compelled to do, but I thought them unnecessary as a source of revenue." As a result, Chapman said he proposed to the other council members, "that if they would refuse to grant licenses I would make good any deficit in revenue needed by the city. This proposition was accepted and Fullerton had no saloons until the repeal of the national prohibition law. It is interesting to note that I had no deficit to make up."

In the 1906 election the electors voted against the issuance of liquor licenses, 197 to 111, and voted in the "Progressive Citizens Party" ticket with John R. Gardiner being reelected and Clinton H. Smith and George C. Welton joining the council (Amerige was defeated and Dr. Clark had moved out of town) with Benchley and Chapman, whose terms carried over. The *Fullerton News* proclaimed:

> "Monday was a day that marked an epoch in the history of the city of Fullerton that will not soon be forgotten, for on that day, we hope, was buried beyond resurrection the bitter animosities and jealousies that have held this city in its throes for a long time. Progression won out and won out handsomely.
>
> "As soon as the result of the vote was announced, the lid came off, and for several hours the city went wild with glorification over the victory. Bonfires were lit, and fireworks galore filled the air, turning the darkness into light. Cannons boomed as long as powder held out, whistles blew as long as there was steam in the boiler, and bells rang till the ropes wore out. Nearly everybody joined in celebrating and Young America was especially happy. It was a fitting climax to a glorious victory."

As the *News* noted, relationships among city leaders had been acrimonious, an example being made public in the *Tribune* on March 1, 1906, just before the 1906 election, when headlines on a council meeting story proclaimed "Trustee Amerige Grossly Insulted by Czar Chapman, the 'Great I Am' — Hot Meeting." The story reported several differences of opinion involving Edward R. Amerige on one side and E. K. Benchley and Chapman on the other. It quoted Chapman as accusing Amerige of being a "born kicker," with Benchley agreeing and Amerige saying "People have a right to kick some times . . ." Chapman said, "Amerige, you are a burden to the city," to which Amerige responded, "So are you."

The *Tribune* jumped into the fray, leaving no question where it stood:

> "Czar Chapman also intimated that the city would be better off without Mr. Amerige. How is that, coming from the chairman of the board? Amerige is the only member of the board that has the backbone to offer an opinion or express himself or to speak for the people, and when he dares to express is honest opinion, he is grossly insulted by a little czar who is worshipped by a few weaklings in Fullerton."

The *Tribune*'s outburst was hardly a surprise to Chapman, who said in his autobiography, "for a time almost every issue of the *Tribune* had some scurrilous reference to me . . . in referring to Chapman Avenue, he spoke of it as the 'King's Highway,' and to me personally as the 'Czar.'" This attitude by Edgar Johnson, which Chapman said resulted from Johnson's opposition to Chapman's "program of a saloonless city," was one of the reasons Chapman started an opposition

George Amerige said in a story written in 1937 that it was he who "installed the first water system" on the Fullerton townsite, "employing Chinamen to do the excavation work on the ditches. Hooker Bros. supplied the water pipes and made the connections." In 1904, a special edition of the Fullerton News *included a photo similar to the one here, identifying it as the "Plant of the Fullerton Water Co." and saying it was managed by Frank Griffith. This photo of the same site—but apparently taken slightly later—is identified as the City Water Works of E. A. Honey. Photo courtesy of Launer Local History Room, Fullerton Public Library*

Fullerton gained its first "real" library in 1907 via grants from the Carnegie Foundation. The "Carnegie Library" was built on property purchased at the northwest corner of Pomona and Wilshire avenues—the site of Fullerton's Public Library for the next sixty-six years. The building, facing onto Wilshire Avenue, opened in December 1907. Photo courtesy of Launer Local History Room, Fullerton Public Library

Demand for library services grew with construction of the Carnegie Library. As a measure to relieve the load, a separate cottage was constructed on Wilshire Avenue adjacent to the west end to house children's library services. The building is now in Hillcrest Park where it houses Red Cross activities. Photo courtesy of Launer Local History Room, Fullerton Public Library

newspaper. Happily, however, the Chapman-Johnson relationship eventually changed. Quoting Chapman:

"As an interesting and enjoyable sequel . . . I am pleased to say that later Johnson and I became good friends and through his paper he often expressed his regards."

The feud, however, may have been costly for Fullerton and a boon to Los Angeles. Chapman concluded his story about the reconciliation with this statement:

"However, before this rapprochement, his persistent attacks in the press discouraged my very real desire to give my enthusiastic attention to building up Fullerton, and I turned to Los Angeles, a far more inviting field for major investments."

The election did not end debate over saloon licenses and alcohol in general, an issue which often divided the city and was a central issue in elections extending into the twenties.

Library

But all was not acrimony in 1906. Among major accomplishments was formation of the Library Board of Trustees and the initiation of efforts resulting in construction of Fullerton's first library. Mr. and Mrs. James Dean had moved from Fullerton in 1903, but Mrs. Dean had selected a committee of dedicated women to keep up the work of the reading room in the Chadbourne Building. Josephine (Mrs. Otto) des Granges, Mrs. George W. Sherwood, Mrs. Joseph Goodman, Anna McDermont, and Mrs. Emma Schulte were the members of this group and were joined by Mrs. George Amerige, Mrs. T. B. Van Alystine, Mrs. Cusick, and Mrs. George Weiser in supplying volunteer hours, according

Efforts to get the Federal Public Works Administration involved in the building of a new library for Fullerton were initiated in 1938, but did not come to fruition until 1940. Harry K. Vaughan designed the WPA-constructed building, which remains in use today as the Fullerton Museum Center. The building was dedicated in three days of ceremonies on January 22–24, 1942. Photo courtesy of Launer Local History Room, Fullerton Public Library

to a 1932 *News-Tribune* article written by Suzanne Clair Dean. In June the City Council selected the first library trustees, including J. C. Braley (president), W. W. Kerr (secretary), William Crowther, Alex McDermont, and J. E. Ford. McDermont and Crowther resigned in July, McDermont having moved away and Crowther having been named to the City Council, and A. L. Vincent and D. R. Callings filled the vacancies.

Talk of seeking Carnegie fund aid for construction of a library building began almost immediately and, before the year was out, a grant of $7,500 had been approved by the Carnegie Foundation. In January 1907, another $2,500 was requested and approved, and the lot at the northwest corner of Wilshire and Pomona was purchased. Building plans were accepted in April, a construction contract ($9,397) awarded in May, a librarian Minnie Maxwell—appointed in June (at a salary of $50 per month) and, on November 25, the completed building was accepted by trustees. On December 16, 1907, a gala public reception marked the opening of Fullerton's first library building, the Carnegie Library which housed 859 books—162 contributed as a nucleus by the reading room, 178 donated by the Fullerton Library Association and 519 which had been purchased—a small collection of magazines, donated newspapers, and a clipping collection. Mrs. William (Flora) Starbuck, whose Gem Pharmacy in 1888 housed the first books available to the public, was the first card holder; total circulation the first year was 14,690, an average of 45 daily.

The library building opened in 1942 now houses the Fullerton Museum Center, sponsors of this pictorial history. Since 1974 the Museum Center has offered a "unique and diverse program of exhibitions, education activities and cultural events in science, history and art." The building, renovated in 1986, is a designated historical landmark and is as much a part of the cultural scene as the exhibitions it hosts in its three galleries. The Museum Store offers gifts and special items relating to current exhibitions and the facility also has a lecture room with a stage. The center further serves the public by offering both indoor and outdoor rental space. Photo by the author

High School

There was also activity on the school front in 1906. High School District Trustees, paying heed to a rise in enrollment from the eight of 1893 to sixty-two in 1906, awarded a contract for construction of a new high school building. On May 3 the *Fullerton News* announced the site had been chosen by a vote of the people, the choice being the "Amerige lot on Commonwealth avenue, known as acreage lot

A sparkling new Fullerton Public Library opened in June 1973, on a site west of the new Fullerton City Hall. The 50,000-square-foot, split-level edifice cost $1.36 million. Photo by the author

The Fullerton Tribune *probably got its start in April 1893. The two-story, wood-frame building pictured here—reportedly built late in 1893—was its second home (the first of its own) and also the home (upstairs) of the Edgar Johnson family. The* Tribune's *third home was a brick-front structure with large windows at 107 South Spadra, constructed and occupied in 1904. Photos courtesy of Launer Local History Room, Fullerton Public Library*

62, containing nearly four acres." That site, now Amerige Park, garnered 127 votes, as compared to 62 for the old school site at Wilshire and Lawrence, one for the "Porter site" south of the railroad tracks, and two for the "Ruddock site" on Wilshire. In September the *Tribune* reported a contract had been "let for erection of the new Union High School building, it being awarded to Crookshank & Somers of Los Angeles on a bid of $42,749, which was the lowest of the six bids submitted." The structure was to be 132 by 136 feet in size and contain twenty-one rooms, "one of the handsomest and most modern high school buildings in the state."

The high school moved into its new—but ill-fated—quarters in the fall of 1908. Here were "facilities only dreamed of on the old site," said Louis Plummer, including new laboratories, a gymnasium in the basement, an athletic field, central heating plant, and nice offices. And, it was only a start. By 1910 trustees realized more facilities were needed and plans were made for construction of a new polytechnic building to house woodwork and machine shops, a foundry, and cooking, sewing, and art classes. Contracts totaling more than $18,000 were let in June and the building was ready in November, with formal acceptance scheduled for November 19.

And then tragedy.

Plummer wrote the following: "During the early morning hours of November 18, people of the district watched the fire department of Fullerton futilely attempt to fight back flames of unknown origin that consumed their high school building. By daybreak all that was left of it were a few charred timbers, foundation, a tall smokestack, and a little equipment saved from the domestic science and manual training rooms in the basement."

The good news was that the new Polytechnic Building had been spared, and it, along with four huge tents and, later, bungalows, were to house Fullerton's high school students for the next three years until new facilities could be built.

There was considerable debate about where to build the new school, and at one time in early 1912 the high school district actually owned three potential sites. The old site on Commonwealth was first favored, but rejected because of the train noise. The next favored site, 14.13 acres on Chapman Avenue about a mile east of Harbor—the Hilliard tract—was considered "too far out of town" by many. The third site was located a block east of Harbor in the "Central Tract." In the end, after injunctions and other court action, it was the voters of the district who decided on the Central Tract site, which cost the district $25,716. Plans originally drawn for the Hilliard site were adapted to the new location and the Polytechnic Building was moved there and classes on the new campus began in 1913. The Hilliard tract was sold to two private parties (including the school principal, Delbert Brunton) and the Commonwealth site was sold to the city for use as a park.

Elementary Schools

The elementary school district was not standing idly by while all this was happening. In January 1906, enrollment had risen to 281 pupils, so, in July of that year, when the high school district had made clear its intentions to build a new school, the elementary trustees voted to to purchase the former high school building at the corner of North Lawrence and Wilshire avenues. In 1907, the elementary schools got their first telephones and eight teachers were employed.

After this flurry of activity, more followed in the century's second decade. In February 1913, the old building (former high school building) at the corner of Lawrence and Wilshire was torn down and a new twelve-room school, known as the Wilshire Avenue School, was built and occupied in 1914. By 1915 there were sixteen teachers employed and, by 1919, full-time home economics and manual training departments had been added. Average daily attendance heading into the third decade of the century had increased to 486 and trustees proceeded to purchase the twelve lots between Harvard (Lemon), Lawrence, Chapman, and Whiting avenues that were not already school property. The district was now poised for expansion in the building boom of the 1920s.

Fullerton's first hospitals were located in the central area of the city and the second one ever built is still standing today. The first hospital, completed in August 1903, was a two-story wood-frame structure resembling a large mansion. It was built at the northeast corner of Amerige and Pomona avenues and Charles C. Chapman was the chairman of the Board of Directors which included Dr. C. L. Rich, B. C. Balcom, William Starbuck, Dr. D. W. Hasson, Dr. William Freeman, and Dr. George C. Clark. The second Fullerton Hospital was built in 1915 on the same site, and the building remains today in the hands of a private social services agency. Photos courtesy of Launer Local History Room, Fullerton Public Library

Improvements

City trustees had taken steps immediately after the incorporation election to solidify the business base of the downtown area. In September 1904, the *Tribune* announced, "FULLERTON WILL HAVE NEW CEMENT SIDEWALKS AND CURBS," explaining that trustees had approved construction, despite protests from Carrie Ford, Mrs. James Vail, and William Starbuck (road construction was often hotly debated in the fledgling city).

Building had continued in the downtown area, including the Dean Block, which is still standing today and is considered by most as the oldest extant commercial structure in Fullerton. The Dean Block, at what is now 111–113 North Harbor, was built (C. E. Holcomb said the original building was moved to the site from the ghost town of Carlton near Yorba Linda, but current authorities question this) in phases between 1899 and 1901, when it was occupied by the Dean Hardware Company, which quickly became a leading hardware dealer in the county.

On the spiritual side, the Methodists—First Methodist Episcopal Society—opened their sparkling new brick edifice at the southwest corner of Amerige and Pomona avenues with gala dedication ceremonies—"a very pleasing experience," the *Fullerton News* reported—on a crisp Sunday at the end of November 1909. The "new and imposing church" was 40 by 82 feet in size and its interior included two large memorial windows, one dedicated to the memory of F. R. Holcomb, founding pastor the church, and the other to Miss Lula Collins, donated by her family. The solid, stately building has housed several different religious denominations through the years and stands today on its original site, still serving parishioners.

Walter P. (Big Train) Johnson pitched a record twenty-one consecutive seasons with the Washington Senators, 1907 through 1927, but before that the big man from Olinda was the ace of the Fullerton Union High School staff. Johnson is seen in two photos, first with his high school classmates (fifth from the left in the top row) and again striking a pose in his Washington Senators uniform. The Baseball Hall of Fame right-hander had an overall record of 416 wins and 279 losses (leading the American League in games won for six seasons and winning 20 or more games in ten consecutive seasons). Johnson started 666 games for the Senators and completed 521. He pitched 5,924 innings, including eighteen years of 200 or more innings while leading the league five years in innings pitched. Johnson was followed into the major leagues by another from Fullerton High School, Hall of Famer J. Lloyd (Arky) Vaughan who set National League records with the Pittsburgh Pirates and later the Brooklyn Dodgers. Vaughan, who died tragically in a drowning incident, had a lifetime batting average of .318 over fourteen seasons in the major leagues, leading the league in hitting and slugging percentage in 1935 at .385 and .607 respectively. Photos courtesy of Launer Local History Room, Fullerton Public Library and Cooperstown National Baseball Hall of Fame

Fire Department

Seven years after the Dean Block opened, it—and the whole of downtown Fullerton—was almost lost to flames. Three structures at the southwest corner of Amerige and Harbor—the McDermont Block and the Gregg and Denkle buildings—burned to the ground on April 10, 1908, in an incident that mobilized Fullerton's citizenry and resulted, four months later, in the creation of the Fullerton Fire Department.

"Had the wind been blowing, it is believed the whole business part of town would have been consumed by the fire, as the city has absolutely no fire protection," the *Orange County Tribune* reported. "As the flames were rapidly spreading, men broke into the two buildings (where Nancy Gregg, former postmaster, and the six-member family of shopkeeper E. J. Denkle lived) to notify those of the danger. It was ascertained that Miss Gregg was spending the night with a friend in the country . . . E. J. Denkle, wife, and four small children, were aroused and got out of their building just as it commenced to burn, and lost everything, except the piano. . . ."

The day of the fire a committee met to discuss fire protection in the community and, on April 17 filed a report. The group cited a plan for obtaining water, recommended purchase of 1,200 to 1,500 feet of hose ("of good quality" costing about 85 cents per foot) and announced that between $1,500 and $1,600 had already been subscribed to by community businessmen. The committee noted the following costs for initiating fire protection: "Hose, $1,200; hose carts, $250; three nozzles, $25; hook and ladder, $475, 60-gallon chemical fire engine, $385; two hand extinguishers, $25; fire bell, $30; store house, $150; installing two fire plugs for temporary system, $150." From that point matters moved swiftly and by August 5, 1908, the *Tribune* reported the enrollment of volunteer fire company members, who chose Emerson J. Marks—the city attorney—as chairman of their group and O. J. Harvey as secretary. The organizing committee included August "Gus" Stern, August Hiltscher, Dr. Jessie Chilton, W. P. Scobie, and O. J. Harvey. Later Chilton was elected president, J. G. Delozier, vice president; O. J. Harvey, secretary; John R. Gardiner, treasurer; O. S. Erickson, chief; Emerson J. Marks, first assistant chief; and Gus Stern, second assistant chief of the first Fullerton Fire Department.

Early arrivals in the Fullerton area remarked that the area's plant life included castor bean trees, and this one, on Santa Fe Avenue, attests to their size. This picture was reportedly taken in 1905 and the woman in the foreground of the photo has been identified as Mrs. "Candy" White. The child standing on one of the tree's lower limbs was not identified. Photo courtesy of Launer Local History Room, Fullerton Public Library.

Police Department

Some have held that law enforcement began with the town's founding, but, in fact, it was some time later, not until "township" status was granted and constable A. A. Pendergrast was appointed. Many breathed a sigh of relief, as lack of "the law" had been a concern. Witness the following from the July 29, 1893 *Fullerton Tribune*:

"*A number of roughs, hailing from everywhere, make it a point to come to Fullerton every Sunday and after imbibing a liberal quantity of tarantula juice proceed to paint the town a bright, brilliant carmine tint. They do this with the*

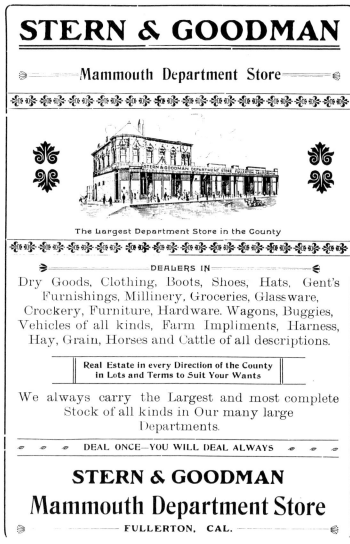
An advertisement in the special "illustrated" edition of the Fullerton News *published January 2, 1904, contained a fine drawing of the Stern and Goodman store at the southeast corner of Spadra (Harbor) and Commonwealth avenues and its listing of services and goods offered provides proof of its standing as the area's top merchant. Photo courtesy of Launer Local History Room, Fullerton Public Library*

knowledge that we have no peace officer in this section, and accordingly they have no fear of arrest. We need a constable and a justice of the peace. Anaheim, a small village south of here, has two of each."

Presumably, the presence of a constable reined in the "roughs," even though the "police department" was basically a one-man affair, with the exception of times when a "deputy" or "assistant" was around, such as James Gardiner, the deputy constable who died following the 1900 flood. This changed with incorporation of the city, when law enforcement took an official step forward with the election of W. A. Barnes as city marshal. Barnes, reconfirmed as marshal in the April 1904 election, was also the street superintendent for the new city, however, and, because of the burdens of handling two jobs, he resigned the marshal's post in June of that year.

A history of the department written by Philip A. Goehring, Fullerton's chief from 1987 until retirement at the end of 1992, tells us Charles E. Ruddock (who lost both 1904 elections) was appointed to succeed Barnes in July 1904, and was subsequently elected to the post in 1906 and 1908. In 1910, Roderick D. Stone was elected marshal and, in 1912, William French was named his deputy, taking over in November when Stone resigned. The marshal and his deputy put on uniforms for the first time in July 1914, and a new jail was built in 1916, the same year city trustees agreed to spend $2.50 for a badge for French "provided he wears it outside his coat."

Among pre-1920s highlights cited by Chief Goehring were the naming of thirty-five citizens as deputies to help when needed (sort of a reserve force); the partial burning of the jail in 1916; the first "motorcops" in 1918 (the same year Vernon "Shorty" Myers was elected marshal); and, in 1919, the installation of a fingerprinting system and the building of a new City Jail on the City Hall grounds. Goehring's history also lists Myers as the first with the title of "chief" and there have been just ten successors to that position since. The department boasted about five officers in 1920, but the Roaring Twenties were upon us and changes were a certainty.

Oil

Oil was discovered in the region in the 1890s, but the Fullerton oil fields, literally the life blood of the community through its formative years, sprang to the fore in 1906 with a series of gushers brought in by Simon J. Murphy on the former Bastanchury properties. Spawned by the fossils of sea creatures described in the opening chapter of this book, oil in rich quantities lay beneath the surface—at about three thousand feet—of the Coyote Hills. Murphy's driller, Lew Bauer, found it in about 1904, after first drilling through mineral hot springs. The well was taped, as discussed earlier, and no one was told of the discovery.

In 1905, Murphy purchased more than 2,200 acres of the Bastanchury ranch at about $35 per acre; in October 1906, two gushers came in, followed by many fine wells followed over the years, many still operating. The 1906 discoveries brought prospectors out in full strength—"In six days following Murphy's successes, nearly 1,000 acres changed hands," Esther Cramer reported in *La Habra, The Pass Through The Hills.* Many established firms, like Union Oil Company, which also explored and developed the Bastanchury lands, were included in the rush for "black gold" riches. Oil revenues would sustain Fullerton government for the next forty years, as explained in an article published by *Architectural Forum* magazine in April 1956:

> "Even the discovery of oil . . . scarcely disturbed the city's sommolence. It was an unexpected dividend; that was all. The city fathers legislated themselves a hefty slice—by 1950, oil revenues accounted for 40 percent of Fullerton's income. . . ."

It changed after that, as people inundated the area in the fifties and oil revenues began to dip. It was time, then, to seek other revenue sources. But, the foundation for Fullerton's growth was built on a forty-year-plus run of financial sustenance from the fossil fuel, even as shipments of citrus and other local products kept the rail cars full.

Fullerton College

The story of Fullerton was headlined "Groves of Academia" in *LEGACY/The Orange County Story,* the seventy-fifth anniversary publication of the *Orange County Register* published in 1980. Education had, indeed, been a prime concern of Fullerton citizenry since the very early days of the community's founding, a concern personified in the story of Fullerton College, "the oldest continually operating community college in the state," which opened its doors to students in September 1913.

Louis Plummer says Delbert Brunton, principal of Fullerton Union High School, recommended, on April 18, 1913, that the Board of Trustees authorize two years of postgraduate work under terms of a state law passed only six years earlier. On April 25, Trustee William Hale moved "that a two-year postgraduate course be added to the curriculum," Plummer reports, and the motion carried unanimously "with the understanding that such work would be offered beginning in September of the next school year." Prices of $10 for each course ($20 for science courses) were established, but later rescinded, and twenty-eight students registered for the first class, which, on September 25, met and selected Earl Dysinger as president; Marjorie Bishop, vice president; Willo Edwards, secretary; and John Rabb, treasurer, of the first ever "FJC" student body.

The "junior college" offered classes in English and Logic, Art, German and Spanish, Mathematics and Science, History, Latin,

The Fullerton Tribune *announcement of cityhood for Fullerton was rather inglorious—a one-column heading on page 1 of the paper's January 28, 1904, edition which was completely overshadowed by the advertising surrounding it. "VOTERS FAVOR CITY" said the headline—next to a two-column headline in larger type proclaiming "OUR GREAT ANNUAL CLEAN UP SALE" in the ad from W. R. Collis where you could buy their regularly priced $12.00 suit for $9.60 and $6.00 suit for $4.80. Shoe sale prices ranged from the highest at $3.00 per pair (regularly $3.75) to the lowest at $1.60 (regularly $2.00). By the way, H. M. Friedman, located in the Masonic Building in the northwest corner of Spadra (Harbor) and Amerige, offered the "Mostest for the Leastest—Your Money's Worth or Your Money Back." Photo courtesy of Launer Local History Room, Fullerton Public Library*

and Manual Training while social events included basketball games with the YMCA, baseball with the Los Angeles Schoolmaster's Club, play production, and student government. Half of the first freshman class returned the next year and were joined by twenty-six new freshman; the year after that enrollment reached forty-four and the following year there were sixty students on the roll. Fullerton College, as an adjunct to the high school, was off and running.

Pacific Electric

Some of the favorite pictures of early Fullerton center on the overpass of Spadra Road (Harbor Boulevard) by the Pacific Electric Railroad and the "Big Red Cars" which transported residents between here and Los Angeles—and other points—via a rapid transit system many wish was still in existence today.

The Pacific Electric Railway was the scheme of Henry Huntington—"conceived, founded, financed and developed," says *Legacy*—who had been spurned in his efforts to assume control of Southern Pacific and decided to start a railroad of his own in 1900. Huntington developed it first in Los Angeles County, then to Orange County in 1904 with a spur to Pacific City—which soon became Huntington Beach—and then branches to Newport Beach (1905), Santa Ana (1907), La Habra (1908), Brea—then Randolph—(1910) and Yorba Linda (1911). A great deal of politicking by Whittier and La Habra merchants preceded the routing to La Habra—and lack of extension to Fullerton. Newspaper articles in 1907 had speculated the railway's arrival in Fullerton was imminent, but it was years before construction actually began on a Fullerton spur.

The Fullerton line, according to a *La Habra Star* article on July 27, 1916, would run "south from La Habra depot through J. G. Launer's ten acres, then south on the east line of Chas. Varney's place, then in a southeasterly direction to the D. [Dominic] J. Bastanchury ranch and through the Bastanchury ranches into Fullerton." The work started in January and continued through 1917 with "a large camp that resembles a town in itself . . . established on the Bastanchury ranch for the men and teams doing the work. . . ." In November 1917, it was announced that "With the construction train crossing the bridge on North Spadra and the track and poles in place to Commonwealth it is assured that the P.E. railroad service will soon be opened to Fullerton." Service actually began February 1, 1918, the big red car coming in from the north through the Bastanchury ranch and then following a route roughly approximating Berkeley Avenue as it crossed the bridge and circled down just east of Lawrence Avenue to about Santa Fe, then westward before looping up to the depot at 136 East Commonwealth Avenue—the very building which today houses Il Ghiotto Italian Restaurant.

In honesty, the passenger line into Fullerton never did achieve success (even though it was popular for the young suitors of the day to take their dates on midnight excursions to the theater in Los Angeles), but the freight line did much the tracks remained in place for years (an anniversary excursion occurring on the line as late as 1952) and freight was shipped over the rails through the 1950s. The landmark Harbor Boulevard overpass was removed in 1964.

World War I

Much of the latter part of the period covered in this chapter, in the era preceding the city's first building boom, the concentration of residents was focused on something completely outside Fullerton's boundaries. It was the First World War. "There are no service flags for those at home, but in shouldering the burdens over here they are displaying the same fine and resistless spirit of patriotism as are their loved ones who are shouldering muskets over there," the *Los Angeles Examiner* wrote in a special booklet entitled *Anaheim and Fullerton's Part in the World War, 1918.* Among other matters, the booklet reported:

"Early in September 211 men had donned the uniform and a large proportion were in the front lines on the battle fields of France. . . . And all of these . . . were as fine young men in their enthusiasm and character as ever went out from American homes to fight the supreme battle for the liberties of the world.

"Fullerton has given unusual impetus and force to her war activities through the Fullerton Club, an organization with more than 200 members. Fifty-four of these have entered the service.

"The city has gone over the top in every [Liberty Bond] drive. The first Liberty Loan brought $75,000, the second $350,000, and the third $245,000. In the War Savings campaign $90,000 was realized. Twenty-seven thousand dollars was contributed to the Red Cross, $22,000 to the Y.M.C.A., and $1,500 to the Y.W.C.A.

"The Fullerton Red Cross chapter has seven auxiliaries. These had shipped, in the period from January to June, 1918, 65,879 surgical dressings, 1,584 knit garments and 740 hospital garments."

Also on the home front, it was reported that the city's churches had given generously to Armenian relief and support of an orphanage in France; that the Board of Trade had entertained with a dinner and royal sendoff for every contingent of "selects" heading to camp; the Home Guard escorted them to the station and the Red Cross provided comfort bags to each and every serviceman. All this says nothing of citizen participation in "the war garden campaign to the ultimate."

And as the war drew to a halt, Fullerton prepared for expansion. Postwar United States was hungry, and Fullerton ranchers were ready to supply them with all the citrus products, fruit, and vegetables they could use; and postwar United States was mobile, creating a need for the petroleum products surging from the Fullerton oil fields; and a new westward movement was beginning. Fullerton was poised on the brink of a boom.

Students arrive for classes at the "new" high school building on West Commonwealth Avenue (where Amerige Park is now located aboard a horse-drawn "school bus" (relatives informed the author that the driver of the bus is Lloyd N. Cookson). Construction of this building was prompted by a rapid increase in high school enrollment and indications that much more was to come in the wake of cityhood for Fullerton. Photo courtesy of Launer Local History Room, Fullerton Public Library

(Facing page top and left) These scenes greeted Fullerton's citizens on the morning of November 18, 1910, after an early morning blaze of undetermined origin swept through the two-year-old high school building on West Commonwealth Avenue in what is now Amerige Park. The first photo looks to the southeast, the second to the north. Later, four tents, and still later, wooden bungalows, were erected on the site to house classes during the two years it took to decide on a new campus location and construction of six buildings there. Photos courtesy of Launer Local History Room, Fullerton Public Library

There was great debate before the site for a new high school was selected, but finally acreage in what was known as the Central Tract on Chapman Avenue just a block east of Spadra (Harbor). The site has been home to Fullerton High School ever since. This photo—retouched with landscaping drawn in so it could be used as a postcard—shows the original campus (note the Polytechnic Building from the Commonwealth site at the left center). Photo courtesy of Launer Local History Room, Fullerton Public Library

The mode of transportation for high school students had moved into the motorized age as this photo of a gasoline-powered school bus attests. You will note that it was a drafty ride in winter and the student—and driver—are bundled up against the elements in heavy coats and lap robes. Photo courtesy of Launer Local History Room, Fullerton Public Library

Fullerton pioneer John H. Clever is shown in front on his ranch residence at what is now 630 West Commonwealth Avenue in this photo from the family album. Notes on the back of the photo written by Clever's son, Otis Howard Clever, indicate the picture was taken in 1912. Photo courtesy of the author, from the Verna Lumbard collection contributed by the Clever family

John R. Gardiner's blacksmith shop in the 100 block of West Commonwealth Avenue was a thriving business for the man who was the leading vote-getter in the first election of a Fullerton Board of Trustees (City Council) in 1904. So successful was the business, which branched out into wagon and farm implement construction, that Gardiner decided in 1913 to expand. He built the new building up around the old wooden frame structure (you can see the start of construction at the left and right of the top picture) so that there would be no loss of business, and when the new building was ready, they simply demolished the old. Photo courtesy of Launer Local History Room, Fullerton Public Library

The Fullerton Military Band, an award-winning group of musicians in which the entire community took pride, posed for this picture in front of the Richman home on West Commonwealth Avenue in about 1908, a year after the band was organized. Identified are (standing, from left, back row) A. W. Koch, Elmer Ford, Byron Richman, Harry Inskeep, Herbert Salverson, William Lindhurst, Charles Lloyd, Henry Dyckman, Guy Pickett, W. B. Potter, Fred Bernstein, Harry Swan, Roy Gibson, and Matthew Shill. Kneeling, from left, are Glenn Stilwell, Lucien Rogers, William Tracy, Milo French, C. E. Ruddock, Bennet Schultz, Willard Rogers, Edward Engman, and Lloyd Emerick. Seated in front are Lucien Edwards, Charles Garringan, Harry Schriver (leader), William McEachran, and Otto Dyckman. Photo courtesy of Launer Local History Room, Fullerton Public Library

This is Fullerton's first "fire station." The shed was built to house fire equipment for Fullerton's volunteer department which was formed in 1908 after a fire leveled three buildings in the downtown section. Photo courtesy of Launer Local History Room, Fullerton Public Library

It was a sure sign of progress when Fullerton's downtown streets were first paved. Sidewalks and curbs had been added to the downtown area soon after incorporation in 1904, and the streets had been watered, compacted, and oiled to hold the dust down in summer and keep them mud-free in winter. It was not until 1913 that paving was actually installed. This photo, looking to the south, shows the street crew laying down the gravel base and asphalt in the 100 block of South Spadra (Harbor). Photo courtesy of Launer Local History Room, Fullerton Public Library

Fullerton, old-timers have said, always enjoyed a celebration. The Fourth of July was an occasion for a downtown parade. This photo, which has been identified as a parade on July 4, 1912, appears to have been taken from atop the Stern and Goodman Building and looks to the northwest at the 100 block of North Spadra (Harbor), showing the Chadbourne Building and the Dean Block on the left side of the picture, as well as the Masonic Building (Book Harbor) a block away (center of photo). It is particularly interesting to note the absence of paving on Spadra and the mixture of horse-drawn and gasoline-powered vehicles. Photo courtesy of Launer Local History Room, Fullerton Public Library

The late Otto Evans remains today a much recognized and unabashed booster of Fullerton and needy causes. For years Otto organized the Salvation Army's Christmas Kettle Fund Drive in Fullerton and boosted the Kiwanis Club's Boy Scout Breakfast, now held in conjunction with Founder's Day (he even sold tickets to complete strangers while vacationing in Hawaii). But before taking up charitable causes and helping feed and clothe the needy, Otto was a businessman in downtown Fullerton, operating a candy shop/cafe/soda foundation at the northeast corner of Amerige and Spadra (Harbor). He is pictured behind the counter of his sweet shop in a photo reportedly taken in 1914. Photo courtesy of Launer Local History Room, Fullerton Public Library

The Hetebrink House at 515 East Chapman Avenue, abutting the campus of Fullerton College at Berkeley Avenue, is a beautifully maintained monument to the past. The Mission Revival/Moorish style, two-story home (seen here in an early photo) was built by the Hetebrink family in 1914 and remains occupied by a Hetebrink at this writing. Albert "Pete" Hetebrink was fifteen when this family moved into the home, the hub of what was then a forty-acre tomato—later, orange—ranch; in 1992, at the age of ninety-two, Pete Hetebrink—with his sister, Mrs. Dorothy Theaker—graciously greeted guests visiting his home as Fullerton Heritage members hosted this venue of the YWCA House and Garden Tour. Fullerton Heritage is supporting efforts to gain Local Landmark Status for the Chapman Avenue home. Photo courtesy of Launer Local History Room, Fullerton Public Library

There's another "Hetebrink House" in Fullerton, but it is not seen as frequently as the Chapman Avenue residence and is now known as "Titan House" because the brick structure on the campus of California State University, Fullerton, served as the administration offices of the CSUF football team. The home was once that of the Henry T. Hetebrink family (a son, John W., built the house on Chapman) who operated a dairy farm on the site. Photo by the author

In 1914 a new resource came to the Bastanchury Ranch—clear drinking water. Bastanchury Water remains a viable market commodity today. In this picture, Maria Bastanchury (center) and two of her sons, Josef and Gaston, watch the pumping of the famed drinking water. Photo courtesy of Launer Local History Room, Fullerton Public Library

William Jennings Bryan, three-time Democratic presidential nominee who served as U.S. secretary of state in Woodrow Wilson's administration, visited Fullerton on May 14, 1917. He is seen here (from left are Phillip Goodell, Roy Hale, Ernest Wetzel, Catherine Caldwell, Bryan, Armon "Pat" Sullivan, Leland Pickering, and Elmer Guinn) outside the Hotel Shay (St. George Hotel) in downtown Fullerton, where local alumni of the University of Nebraska and selected guests entertained him at breakfast. Later, the man called "The Great Commoner" by the Fullerton News addressed the student body at the high school. Among quotations the Daily Tribune attributed to Bryan, a man known for his great oratorical abilities, was: "Life is not to be measured by what we get out of the world, but what we put into the world." And, the newspaper said, he also told his audience, "If you say to a man, it is wrong to steal, and he says, 'I don't know,' don't argue with him; search him. You may find the reason in his pocket." Bryan added to his fame in 1925 when he was one of the prosecutors opposing Clarence Darrow at the John T. Scopes evolution trial in Tennessee. Photo courtesy of Launer Local History Room, Fullerton Public Library

Stockholders of the Fullerton Mining and Milling Company are seen preparing for the trip home from Twenty-Nine Palms. It is believed this company—"Shares Now 10¢ Going to 25¢ Soon"—was owned by John R. Gardiner, who, in a 1955 Daily News-Tribune article admitted that he "had taken a flier" with a mining and milling company that "had fizzled out." Photo courtesy of Launer Local History Room, Fullerton Public Library

William Schumacher served on the Orange County Board of Supervisors, representing Fullerton and other cities and communities of the Third District, which then took in all of North Orange County, for many years at the early part of the century. Photo courtesy of Launer Local History Room, Fullerton Public Library

These are the members of the Fullerton Home Guard as they appeared, apparently at City Park (Amerige Park) on Commonwealth Avenue in 1918, according to information supplied with the photo. Photo courtesy of Launer Local History Room, Fullerton Public Library

The student body of Chapman Avenue School in 1928 assembles at the front entrance to the building which once stood at the southeast corner of Chapman and Harvard (Lemon Street) avenues. This school was built in 1920, was reconstructed after the earthquake of 1933, and was then joined by construction of an auditorium to the "new" Wilshire Avenue School at the northeast corner of Wilshire and Harvard. Fullerton College now controls these properties. Photo courtesy of Launer Local History Room, Fullerton Public Library

CHAPTER VIII

The Builders

1920–1950

The decade initiating this period has been called the Roaring Twenties, and in Fullerton it was exactly that. The year 1920 kicked off a thirty-year segment of history which traveled a course from boom to bust, from peace to war and then back again to the cusp of nearly unprecedented growth. It was a period which saw the solid foundation of a city laid firmly in place, materially, socially, philosophically. It was a time of building—structurally, with creation of landmarks still standing, and in character, as the community faced unexpected challenges in both prosperity and despair. When it was over, Fullerton and its people emerged with the moral resolve which continues to guide a still-growing community.

Fullerton was a city of 4,415 people in 1920, enjoying the natural growth that follows incorporation, but, most likely, not prepared for the influx of business and people that would bring Orange County's tallest building, a celebrated hotel, and an exquisite theater to its downtown and boost the population to 10,860 in 1930.

City of Orangethorpe

An early challenge of the twenties had its roots in the sewer—Fullerton's sewer system, that is. In the fall of 1920, a growing Fullerton faced a need for expanded sewage facilities, specifically more land for what was known as a "sewage farm." In August 1920, the *Fullerton Daily Tribune* told of plans to annex land south of the existing "farm" (at the current site of Fullerton Municipal Airport)—and of strong opposition from people in that area. In September, when the city said it was going ahead with plans to provide a place "for the overflow water," area ranchers objected "to what they believe will be an extension of the city sewer farm to their neighborhood." The ranchers succeeded in having the courts void the annexation vote, and, to make sure Fullerton would not try annexation again, they decided to create a city of their own.

On January 7, 1921, voters in the area cast 124 ballots in favor and just 32 against creation of a city named Orangethorpe. The *Tribune* described boundaries of the new city thusly: "[its] northern boundary is also the southern boundary of Fullerton. The western boundary is near Buena Park, the eastern limits near the state highway and the southern boundary near Lincoln avenue." Clarence Spencer

This aerial view shows the campus of Fullerton Union High School to which students moved in the fall of 1913. This photo of the fifteen-acre Chapman Avenue site, dated 1927, was taken before construction of Plummer Auditorium and after construction of the Ebell Club across the street on the northeast corner of Harvard (Lemon) and Chapman (lower/right corner of photo). The Spanish-style arcades had been added to the front of the buildings by the time this photo was taken. Also seen is the Pacific Electric right-of-way at the northern edge of the campus (near top of photo). Photo courtesy of Launer Local History Room, Fullerton Public Library

This view of the high school campus was taken in about 1936, just as construction was beginning on the Fullerton College campus where the land has been cleared and a baseball diamond constructed at its northern edge, just south of the Pacific Electric tracks. The concrete bleachers for the Fullerton High School football stadium have now been installed in a central part of the campus and the baseball field is located where the Fullerton District Stadium is now. The photo also affords another clear view of the Pacific Electric right of way—which marked the eastern edge of the college campus into the mid-1950s. Photo courtesy of Launer Local History Room, Fullerton Public Library

was elected treasurer; L. P. Nichols, city clerk; and the trustees were M. J. Harzler, Herman Allgeyer, S. D. Winters, and J. M. McDuel. Having served its purpose in ending the sewer threat, the City of Orangethorpe disincorporated a few years later and the land eventually came to Fullerton or Anaheim via annexations, except for some pockets of unincorporated county territory which remained for many years.

Even as the threat at its borders was being waged, Fullerton's downtown area was shaping up in a form which, in many ways, remains as you see it today. Among buildings constructed then and remaining today are:

"New" Masonic Temple. Fullerton's Masons met for years in the two-story building they built in 1901 at the northwest corner of Harbor and Amerige before deciding to build at the northwest corner of Chapman and Harbor. The new, $115,000 Masonic Temple, dedicated December 8, 1920, was called "one of the finest on the coast." Today, it awaits new uses and refurbishing plans.

The California Hotel (Villa del Sol). "At its beginnings, the California Hotel had been the biggest news in Fullerton, maybe even all of north Orange county," Don Smith wrote in an in-depth history of the former hotel in *Orange Countiana, Volume IV,* issued by the Orange County Historical Society in 1989. The building at the northwest corner of Wilshire and Harbor—dedicated on January 15, 1923, and housing stores, twenty-two apartments, and fifty-five single rooms—was one of very few built with funds raised by popular subscription, "And most likely, it was also the only one to be built as a replacement for a public comfort station." The pubic restrooms filled a need for area ranch residents facing long trips home. Charles C. Chapman chaired the Fullerton Community Hotel Company (CHC)

9-18-55

formed to sell stock in the venture—and personally pledged $25,000 to get the fund drive started. Villa del Sol came about in 1965.

The Chapman Building. When the California Hotel project was in danger of foundering, Smith said Charles C. Chapman provided some impetus with this statement: "The day the city trustees finally and officially vote to turn the proposed site over to the Community Hotel Company, I will instruct my architect to proceed at once with the building on my property across the street." He was true to his word, and when the hotel land was obtained, architect M. Eugene Durfee went to work designing what became the five-story and basement building at the southeast corner of Wilshire and Spadra (Harbor) which opened in December 1923. Refurbished, it stands proudly serving the community today with Pioneer Bank as prime tenant.

Chapman's Alician Court Theater (Fox Fullerton). As early as August 1922, plans were announced for a $150,000 theater on the east side of North Spadra (Harbor), north of Chapman Avenue, but it was nearly two years—July 1924— before C. Stanley Chapman broke ground for his project. The facility opened May 28, 1925, to a "battery of giant searchlights . . . announcing afar that a work of superb beauty had been completed." J. Charles Thamer, master of ceremonies,

This photo, dated September 18, 1955, is highlighted by evidence of the first Fullerton Junior College construction east of the former Pacific Electric tracks—specifically the gymnasium seen in the upper right quadrant of the photo where even more land has been cleared for future development. The residences along Harvard (Lemon) Street remain, as does the Ebell Club building. The high school campus at the left is also much more clearly defined and a running track has replaced the baseball field at the northern end of the campus. The photo also provides a good view of the Wilshire Junior High School complex (right) and other area development, including First Lutheran Church (lower right corner), and the former Church of Religious Science (lower left area). Photo courtesy of Launer Local History Room, Fullerton Public Library

said the building was, "a shining testimony to the vision of its builders; a real answer to the aesthetic tastes and desires of the people of this community." The building is awaiting plans for refurbishing.

Amerige Block. In 1918 George Amerige sold the St. George Hotel to the Whiting Meade Wrecking Company for $1,300. When the structure, the hub of Fullerton social activities for most of its thirty years, was razed, it paved the way for Amerige to build the series of stores, each styled with different glazed tile facade, extending eastward on the north side of the 100 block of East Commonwealth. This is the "Amerige Block," and a plaque commemorating it has been placed at the northeast corner of Harbor and Commonwealth. Later, early in 1922, Amerige went to the north side of the block and, on 136 feet of frontage extending easterly from the alley on the south side of the 100 block of East Amerige Avenue, constructed five more business buildings. As they were built, a $55,000 facelift was completed on the Farmer's and Merchant's Bank at the southeast corner of Amerige and Harbor (where a more exhaustive renovation was finished in 1991).

Odd Fellows Hall (Williams Company). In 1927 the International Order of Odd Fellows constructed an imposing, three-story brick building on the south side of the 100 block of East Commonwealth, extending eastward from the alley. The lodge's meeting hall—intact today with built-in, tiered seating at the sides, a stage at the rear, and high, arched windows—occupies the rear of the second and third floors, where the secret nature of the society required a viewing slot in the meeting hall's door. This "peep hole" led to speculation that, perhaps, a "speak-

The Pacific Electric Railway viaduct over Spadra Road (Harbor Boulevard) was constructed late in 1917, but during the 1920–1950 period it came to be recognized as a landmark, a welcoming archway to the north end of the downtown area. "Welcome to Fullerton" was written on the north side of the archway; "Fullerton—Come Again" bid a pleasant adieu on the south side of the structure. The signs took on many forms as new coats of paint were applied, but one of the more popular combinations featured bold orange letters outlined in blue with stripes of the same colors at the sides. The landmark became a hazard to the ever increasing size of trucks traveling Spadra, however, and faded to the wrecking ball in 1964. Photos courtesy of Launer Local History Room, Fullerton Public Library

In January of 1917, a local newspaper reported, "George Amerige . . . sold a piece of land opposite Hotel Shay (St. George Hotel) on East Commonwealth Avenue to Edward Engman. This tract will be used for depot purposes." The Pacific Electric Depot was ready for use when the first train pulled in from La Habra on February 1, 1918, and it remains ready for customers of Il Ghiotto Italian Restaurant at this writing. Photo by the author

easy" was housed here during Prohibition, but there is no evidence to support this, and more than one resident has said there were no hidden bars in Fullerton.

Union Pacific Depot (Spaghetti Factory). The Union Pacific, last of three railroads to serve Fullerton, began building its depot south of the tracks on Walnut Avenue in 1916, but suspended construction during World War I. Building resumed in 1922 and the structure, complete with mission tile roof, octagonal dome and round cupola, was finished and placed in service in 1923. In 1980, the Fullerton Redevelopment Agency purchased it and had it moved across the tracks and Harbor Boulevard via the overpass to the new Transportation Center, where it houses the Spaghetti Factory.

California Bungalow Court. Fullerton architect Frank Benchley designed this craftsman style court at 314 North Pomona Avenue, which was built in 1922. There are ten units in the facility, balanced by a two-story structure in the rear and spanned in front by a pergola.

Hotel DeLuxe (Allen Hotel). The Hotel DeLuxe was constructed in 1923. It's twenty second-floor sleeping rooms initially hosted railroad workers on their

In a description of Fullerton's early days written in 1937, George Amerige reported selling the St. George Hotel to make room for "business blocks" which were built in 1919–1920. Those buildings—at the corner (George Amerige and his wife Annette lived in the spacious upstairs apartment for about twenty years) and extending eastward along the north side of the 100 block of East Commonwealth—remain today. One picture shows the corner soon after the business buildings were built, and the other as they appear at this writing. Photos courtesy of Launer Local History Room, Fullerton Public Library, and the author

stopovers in Fullerton, while the downstairs was used for retail businesses. The Hotel DeLuxe became the Deluxe Hotel in 1934 and the Allen Hotel in 1945. The Fullerton Redevelopment Agency acquired the property and has approved a plan which will preserve the structure and add adjacent buildings in a combined residential-commercial development.

"New" Santa Fe Station. Now it is listed on the National Register of Historic Places, but when it was dedicated on July 2, 1930, the "$50,000 edifice" was labeled "a monument to progress." The station, now host to AMTRAK, is poised for new life as the Bushala Brothers, Inc., leaseholders, and the city have agreed on restoration and expansion plans.

Two other buildings of significance still with us today made their appearance in the 1920s, although they are not in what could be termed the "downtown area." They are:

The Muckenthaler Home (Muckenthaler Cultural Center). Walter and Adella Muckenthaler wanted a home that "would be a house for a sunlit land," Keith C. Terry reported in his book *Walter M. Muckenthaler*, a 1974 biography commissioned by Harold M. Muckenthaler and written from interviews conducted for the California State University, Fullerton, Oral History Program. The beautiful Mediterranean style home they helped create with architect Frank Benchley and contractor E. J. Herbert—a 7,600-square-foot structure which took six months to build in 1923 and cost $34,000 ($4.75 per square foot), not including landscaping and furnishings—fulfilled their desires. In 1965, Adella Muckenthaler and her son, Harold, deeded the home and grounds to the city. The center, closed at the end of 1981, was reopened in June 1984 after extensive rehabilitation. Construction of a new 220-seat amphitheater, and of a hospitality center, was completed in late 1992.

Maple School. If current planning comes to fruition, Maple School will return to its original use as an elementary school. The school at Harvard (Lemon) and Maple (Valencia) opened in 1924, joining Ford, Chapman, and Wilshire schools as facilities serving the 1,336 students then enrolled in "grammar" school. In the aftermath of the 1933 earthquake, Maple was reconstructed. In 1972, school trustees adopted a desegregation plan called "The Early Childhood and Community Center Plan," under which Maple students—30 percent of them minorities—were transported to five other schools in the district and Maple became a community center. In 1992, Maple area parents made pleas to have their

What was originally the Christian Science Church at the southwest corner of Pomona and Chapman avenues (142 East Chapman) is a Mission Revival building constructed in 1920, but not dedicated until 1929 when a $35,000 debt had been retired. Experts have noted that the building, now occupied by the Self-Realization Fellowship Church, is distinguished from other Mission Revival buildings by its elaborate relief decoration. Photo courtesy of Launer Local History Room, Fullerton Public Library

What are called "California Bungalow Courts" epitomized development during World War I. The one at 314 North Pomona Avenue remains today, nearly unaltered, as a prime example of this craftsman style of construction. Photo by the author

children attend school in their neighborhood, and school and city were working toward re-establishing a kindergarten through sixth grade facility at Maple School.

In reviewing events like the opening of the California Hotel (January) and the Chapman Building (December), it strikes us that 1923 was a particularly remarkable year in Fullerton building. Other 1923 events included the opening of the new Sitton Garage on the corner of Malden and Commonwealth and, the Ebell Club planning for a new clubhouse at the corner of Harvard (Lemon) and Chapman. Valuation of new building for 1923 was a record-breaking $2,000,000-plus.

All the activity was not downtown, either, as housing construction spread

its wings in all directions. R. S. Gregory and G. W. Finch purchased property at Raymond and Chapman avenues with intent to build homes, and when Anaheim developer Harry Dierker purchased some of the lots and announced a $100,000 project, the *Fullerton Daily Tribune*, April 16, 1923, hailed it the "largest, most comprehensive home building program yet announced in Fullerton." On that same date, the *Tribune* said groundbreaking was held for a two-story apartment building on East Whiting Avenue, "just off Spadra," an E. J. Clarke project containing six single and one double apartment. In August, the paper told of a tract "one of the finest subdivisions yet opened in this vicinity," being developed on twenty acres "on Richman avenue, just off Malvern." The project was being

It was the pride and joy of the community— and it was owned by citizens who purchased shares in the Fullerton Community Hotel Company headed by Charles C. Chapman. Groundbreaking was held January 22, 1922, for the California Hotel at which time corporation board member S. C. Hartranft noted that Fullerton, "already has the finest water system, the finest churches, the best schools, elegant paved streets, a lighting system unequaled anywhere, and civic organizations of which we are proud . . . now we are going to have the finest hotel in the state . . . a triumph without parallel." Dedication ceremonies on January 15, 1923, were attended by large crowds as witnessed by one of the pictures presented here. The three-story building was renamed Villa del Sol in 1965 and in 1992 it was announced plans were being made for another remodeling and earthquake retrofitting. Photos courtesy of Launer Local History Room, Fullerton Public Library, and the author

done by Robert E. Corcoran, "the father of Golden Hill," a location where he and Walter J. Cadman had already subdivided forty acres.

Educational circles were not standing still. A significant—magnificent—building, opened in May 1930, continues to function as a community gathering place. This building, which someone once called "The grand lady of Fullerton," is:

Fullerton Union High School Auditorium (Louis E. Plummer Auditorium). Like a lot of other public construction in Fullerton, the high school auditorium did not experience an easy birthing. Authorization for construction came on a 3–2 vote of high school trustees in October 1928, the objecting trustees having nothing against the auditorium, per se, but, rather, felt construction monies—initially estimated at $200,000 but, in the final

"OPENING OF DEPARTMENT STORE MARKS EPOCH IN DEVELOPMENT OF CITY" read the headline in the Fullerton Daily Tribune *on December 18, 1923, and the Chapman Building, described then as "the finest building of its kind in Orange County," has remained a hallmark of Fullerton's downtown. Ferber's Department Store was the prime tenant, occupying the basement, first floor, mezzanine, and second floor of the 60,000-square-foot building when it opened. Glass bricks in the sidewalk surrounding the structure allowed light to filter into subterranean dressing rooms and the building contained 303,100 common brick. When the $200,000-plus building opened it was the tallest in the county. The Chapman Building (often called the 110 Building—its address is 110 East Wilshire) has undergone a complete retrofitting and refurbishing and at this writing has Pioneer Bank as its prime tenant. These photos show the building at its opening and as it appears today. Photos courtesy of Launer Local History Room, Fullerton Public Library, and the author*

analysis, hitting $295,000—should be focused on building a separate campus for the junior college, then still housed at the high school. Carleton Winslow, Los Angeles architect, headed the project. The building was designated the "Louis E. Plummer Auditorium" at ceremonies in December 1962, which honored the former superintendent of schools. The facility was closed in late 1967 because of earthquake hazards, but was reopened in January 1972, after undergoing a $500,000-plus retrofitting and refurbishing. The "lady" was the subject of a $2.8 million improvement project jointly sponsored by the city and high school district

finished in September 1993, just in time to help celebrate the high school's one hundredth anniversary.

Another highlight—if one dares to call it that—of the 1920s, has to be the strange story of reversed election results and the saga of the "The City Hall That Wasn't":

The City Hall That Wasn't

Fullerton's first City Hall (heretofore, city offices were located in rented offices in the downtown area) was to be located on the west side of Spadra (Harbor) between Wilshire and Whiting avenues. The south portion of this land had been sold for the California Hotel project, but the remainder—where First Interstate Bank and Bank of America are now—

The Rialto Theatre at 219 North Spadra Road (Harbor Boulevard) was the place where Fullertonians watched movies from 1917 to 1927. The Rialto was managed by Harry Wilber, whose daughter, Alice, married Stan Chapman and it was for her that his grand theater was named—Chapman's Alician Court Theater. Photo courtesy of Launer Local History Room, Fullerton Public Library

was still owned by the city. A bond election was held in October 1923, and officials said voters had given the necessary two-thirds majority to the two principal issues, i.e., $160,000 in bonds for the City Hall and $25,000 in bonds for a new firehouse. Voters rejected $15,000 in bonds for equipment, fixtures, and furnishings.

But, the city fathers were happy. They figured a way to get the equipment and furnishings, proceeded to advertise and sell the bonds, then ordered excavation of the site. On November 7, 1923, an architect's rendering of the building, a beautiful structure "Of modified Mission architecture and modeled on distinctive lines," appeared under the heading "Fullerton's City Hall Will Rank With Best." The caption said, "excavation of the site . . . practically completed . . . actual construction will be under way within the next few weeks."

Then came a shocker. There had been a miscalculation. The bonds had not been approved by the voters! There had been a "two-thirds majority of the yeas over the nays" in the voting, but the law read approval must be by two-thirds of the ballots cast. It seems that some had voted on the equipment matter, but not on the construction bonds. Thus, neither of the main issues qualified—the $160,000 issue failed by four votes, the $25,000 issue by sixteen—a fact discovered by attorneys for the companies purchasing the bonds. "Fullerton's immediate prospects for a new city hall are gone aglimmering," said the *Tribune*. "The big hole on the city hall site which had been dug in readiness for the foundations will continue to yawn for some time."

The Spadra site never did house City Hall. But, two-plus years later, in August 1926, Fullerton's city offices were housed in a city-owned building for the first time—upstairs above the brand new Fire Hall on the north side of the 100 block of West Wilshire. They would remain there for sixteen years. The Spadra site was later sold (for $70,000, in what some said was a "secret" deal) for commercial development, the first being a market and the Brown Mug restaurant.

This is how the former Rialto Theatre building looked after its transformation into the First National Trust and Savings. This facade remains today on the building at 219 North Harbor Boulevard. Photo courtesy of Launer Local History Room, Fullerton Public Library

This structure at the northwest corner of Wilshire and Lawrence Avenues replaced the former High School building which had been purchased by the Fullerton School District. The building, with the name Fullerton Grammar School emblazoned on it, was known variously as the Lawrence Avenue School and the Wilshire Avenue School. The school was in service from 1913 until after the earthquake of March 10, 1933, when it was declared unsafe and eventually demolished. Photo courtesy of Launer Local History Room, Fullerton Public Library

Students at Wilshire and Chapman Avenue schools were housed in these temporary quarters—wood floor, rigid tents—following the earthquake of 1933 and rebuilding period which followed, mostly in 1935 and 1936. Photo courtesy of Launer Local History Room, Fullerton Public Library

Fire Hall

We should not pass so lightly over the Fire Hall matter, because the building served as Fullerton's fire headquarters for forty years. Firefighters, the newspaper noted, had a lot to do with that first building, reporting that, "members . . . expended about $400 personally, to furnish their room in the new station." In recognition, city trustees, on July 20, 1926, agreed to spend city funds to purchase "a range for the fire boys." One week later, the *Tribune* announced the station had passed final inspection, was accepted by the city, and occupation was to begin immediately.

City offices moved into the new City Hall the first week of 1942, but fire headquarters remained at 123 West Wilshire Avenue. Modern branch fire facilities were erected—the first being Station No. 2 at Brookhurst Street and Valenica Drive, opened in 1953—to serve outlying areas of the city having high concentration of residential, commercial or industrial uses, but headquarters stayed put until 1966 when the present headquarters station was opened at 312 East Commonwealth Avenue. Today, the fire service network includes the central station and five branch facilities.

Fullerton Rejected by Regents

First, it was no City Hall. Then, in 1925, there was more trauma when an all-out bid to have a branch of the University of California located here—the campus we know as UCLA—was rejected by university regents. Many thought for sure that regents would select the 1,200-acre site on the Bastanchury Ranch. Running from the current Harbor Boulevard west and south to Commonwealth Avenue and Brookhurst Road, the would-be university land was then planted to oranges, lemons, and walnuts, with the exception of a large undeveloped area at the northwest corner.

"Few, if any sites, are available that will surpass the Fullerton location," the Chamber of Commerce said in a brochure issued in December 1924. It then challenged residents to support the bid: "Are you ready to back this up with cash— for the benefit of California, Orange County, and your own community—to make Fullerton the educational center of the southwest?" People responded and newspapers were filled with glowing reports of visits by regents and university administrators. Surrounding communities added support, businesses were ready to make significant contributions, and the city significant concessions, to get the project started. But, on March 21, 1925, the *Tribune* headline read, "FULLERTON SITE REJECTED BY REGENTS." The Board of Regents of the University of California, in session in San Francisco, had decided the new branch would, "be located on the Beverly Hills site in Westwood, a Los Angeles suburb."

This was the look of the reconstructed Maple Avenue School, a one-story edifice instead of the original two-story building built in 1924. Maple School later became Maple Community Center as the school closed as part of a district desegregation plan, but talks have been held about reopening of the facility as— once again—a neighborhood elementary school. Photo courtesy of Launer Local History Room, Fullerton Public Library

This photo, apparently taken from the Chapman Building, clearly shows the excavation north of the California Hotel (left of picture) where the Fullerton City Hall was supposed to be built in 1923. Note the palm trees in the California Hotel block, and the slant parking permitted on Spadra Road (Harbor Boulevard). The Masonic Lodge is visible near the top of this mid-1920s photo, the Pacific Electric viaduct over Spadra can be seen in the distance and the Marwood Apartments at Whiting and Spadra are clearly visible at the upper right. Photo courtesy of Launer Local History Room, Fullerton Public Library

This painting on the side of an old Fullerton fire truck is an architects depiction of what was supposed to be Fullerton's first City Hall. The building was to be built just north of the California Hotel (Villa del Sol) on the west side of Spadra Road (Harbor Boulevard) in late 1923/early 1924. Photo courtesy of Launer Local History Room, Fullerton Public Library

Not all the development of the twenties was downtown . . . the Fullerton community was spreading outward with housing developments, too. Here's an aerial view of the "Golden Hill" development north of what is now Malvern Avenue just after grading was started at the north end of the project headed up by Robert E. Corcoran and Walter J. Cadman. Photo courtesy of Launer Local History Room, Fullerton Public Library

It would take more than thirty years, but eventually Fullerton would become home to a state university.

Fullerton Municipal Airport

Fullerton Municipal Airport is called the "oldest and largest general aviation airfield still in its original location in Orange County," in *Wings Over Fullerton,* a historical pamphlet by Sylvia Palmer Mudrick. As early as 1913, barnstormers and crop-dusters used the site as a landing strip, but it was not until the mid-1920s that steps were taken toward establishment of a permanent facility. Placentia citrus ranchers and pioneer aviators William and Robert Dowling looked beyond the rutted surface of the West Commonwealth Avenue site—once the city's sewer farm and also a pig ranch—and saw its possibilities as an airfield. The brothers enlisted the aide of the Chamber of Commerce in approaching the City Council, and, in January 1927, the Council signed Ordinance 514, leasing the land to the Chamber for five years at a fee of $1 per year. The Chamber subleased operations to William Dowling and a friend, Willard Morris of Yorba Linda. They cleared the surface to create the first formal landing strip and on February 24, 1927, William Dowling piloted a Curtis JN-4D Primary Military Training biplane—a "Jenny"—from Brea Airfield to make the first official landing at Fullerton Airport. "By July, the airport's location was listed on aviation maps," Mudrick wrote, reporting the facility was officially dedicated on April 21, 1928, and the first airshow was held there two days later.

The Chamber maintained its lease on the airport—though subleasees changed—through the 1930s, a period which saw airmail service launched

(1931), the first industrial lease issued (1934—to a manufacturer of metal dirigibles), the first night flights (1938), and the introduction of a Civilian Pilot Training Program (1939, at the James-Colboch Air Service). In January 1941, the city, at the urging of the Chamber, took control of the airport, but after advent of war all civilian flying within 150 miles of the coast was halted and the airport was closed—to civilians, as both Army and Navy pilots used the facility as an auxiliary field and for training.

"When the war ended, the field was returned to the City, along with a new 1,700-foot paved runway," the Mudrick story relates. Then, brothers William and Richard Jewett took an interest and established Fullerton Air Service, which, with Hebert Air Service, handled the twenty five planes based there. Landing lights were added and other improvement made, and by 1948 the number of Fullerton-based planes had grown to two hundred, establishing the pattern for today's eighty-acre facility, with a 3,120-foot runway, room for six hundred aircraft, and an FFA control tower.

The Balboa—Fullerton's own car

But this period in history also involved cars, and one car in particular—Fullerton's own "Balboa." "The Balboa Motor Corporation, whose plant is assured for Fullerton, promises to be the most important manufacturing institution so far acquired for our city." J. C. Bliss of the Fullerton Chamber of Commerce said in the *Tribune* in January 1924. The company displayed a touring car, a sports brougham model and a chassis on the grounds of the California Hotel in

In a photo taken April 8, 1923, the Corcoran Paper Company at 220–222 South Spadra (Harbor) is featured in a photo which also highlights a southbound passenger train stopped at the Fullerton Station. People at the Corcoran building have been identified by members of the Corcoran and Cadman families as (from left, on loading dock) Walter J. Cadman, Lillian Corcoran, Mrs. Cadman (Fern Corcoran), and Robert E. Corcoran and, at the rear of the building, Milton Corcoran. You will also note the Consolidated Ice and Cold Storage Company building (Crescent Ice Company) at the right of photo. Photo courtesy of Launer Local History Room, Fullerton Public Library

March 1924, and announced plans to produce one thousand cars in its first year at a brand-new plant. Stock was sold, plans for a factory displayed, and the prototype autos were showcased at the Ambassador Hotel, Los Angeles, in August 1924, after which the *Los Angeles Times* wrote: "The remarkable performance of the new Balboa motor car, which is guaranteed to deliver twenty-five miles to the gallon of gasoline and which will develop more than 100 horsepower, is entirely due to the supercharged engine." When the cars were shown in March 1925, at the Orange County Auto Show a Continental engine had been substituted for the supercharged straight-eight—and troubles were becoming apparent. Perhaps the ballyhoo was too great, but whatever the reason and despite the positive reception to many of the Balboa's innovations, it failed to make it past the prototype stage and "died a'bornin' " in 1925.

The home of Walter and Adella Muckenthaler, now Fullerton's Muckenthaler Cultural Center, was deeded to the city in 1965 and in 1966 the Cultural Groups Foundation of North Orange County was formed to help fund and operate the facility. Photo courtesy of Launer Local History Room, Fullerton Public Library

And, there are subjects of a less materialistic nature that affected Fullerton and its residents. Not all are pleasant to discuss, but they were part of history and, if not to be dwelled upon at length, they are matters requiring addressing.

The Ku Klux Klan

The presence of the Ku Klux Klan in Fullerton is one of those subjects not often discussed—then, or now. But, the Klan was active in the community, mostly in the first half of the 1920s, and its members included leaders in government, education, business, and religion. It was a different Klan, with different priorities, than most think about when considering the white-hooded claverns of the South. Albert Launer, a former city attorney and School Board member, talked about the Klan in an April 1968 interview with Karol Keith Richard for the California State University, Fullerton, Oral History Programs, giving this assessment of local KKK objectives: "Some of them [Klan members] felt that they could use the Klan to improve and protect . . . youth and the purity of the community. The Klan was apparently presented to the prospective members as an agency through which you could keep this community growing safely and morally, in the right direction." Launer said the Klan included, "a church group, a school group . . . [and] this other group, mainly oil workers." The church/school group, he said, was "tied in with the activities . . . toward good morals and good culture." The oil workers, he believed, "were seeking an opportunity to be part of the enforcement agency."

Klan activities in Fullerton have been charted by Christopher N. Cocoltchos in his exhaustive 1979 UCLA doctoral dissertation, *The Invisible Government And the Viable Community: The Ku Klux Klan in Orange County, California During the 1920s*, as well as in several CSUF Oral History Program interviews with community leaders. Cited in these studies as a particular target of the Klan locally was "John Barleycorn"—alcohol sale and consumption—as well as strong anti-Catholic and anti-Jewish attitudes (though often denied by Klan leaders) and racist feelings, especially as directed toward "Mexicans." However, Fred Strauss told CSUF Oral History Program interviewer Esther Katz in June 1976, "We were Jewish, but they [the KKK] never bothered us any. Some of my best friends belonged and they didn't know what it was all about. . . ." and, Strauss said, after a list of members was obtained, "they came to us, begging for us to scratch their names off the book, because they didn't really want to belong to it; that they were talked into it. They thought it was a new American organization, and so forth."

One Klan incident stands out in Fullerton. Dan O'Hanlon, local Realtor and staunch Irish Catholic, was among five thousand people attending a Klan rally in Amerige Park in June 1924, when he stood up and called the speaker a liar after "unfavorable references to the Catholic Church" were made, according to Cocoltchos. Fullerton police officers stepped in and whisked O'Hanlon away as a crowd, shouting "Get that guy," and "where is a tar bucket," began to encircle him. O'Hanlon was booked for disturbing the peace—charges which were eventually dropped—but that night "a fiery cross was burnt at the O'Hanlon home."

Blacks in Fullerton were not a particular KKK target because they represented less than one-half of 1 percent of Fullerton's male population in 1920 (even less by 1930), and they were not in political posts, nor were they involved in political controversy. These were positions and situations the Klan could use to help "gain control of a community's civic culture." Hispanics—referred to then, always, as "Mexicans"—did draw Klan attention, however, because they were a growing segment of the population (estimated at 3.65 percent of Fullerton males in 1924 and listed at 6.35 percent in the 1930 census) and were—through no actions of their own—involved in civic controversy. Some of these issues are discussed in a separate section to follow.

Most Fullerton residents interviewed as part of the CSUF Oral History Program indicated that many just ignored the Klan. Their opinions were succinctly summarized by the late Superior Court Judge Raymond Thompson in a May 1968 interview with Gerald M. Welt. Thompson said Klan activities divided,

Fullerton residents apparently were enamored of the automobile. From the first appearance of the automobile at the turn of the century, the popularity grew to where photos taken in the mid-1920s show cars and trucks crowding the streets. Fullertonians liked to travel so much that they organized community outings, as seen in one photo presented here where residents are about to leave from in front of the Wickersheim Implement Company on an automobile trip. In another photo, following page, also in front of the Wickersheim store, 100 block West Commonwealth Avenue, vehicles from P. E. Taylor's "Stage" Line are lined up ready to take tourists on trips to several locations, ranging from the desert to the sea. Photos courtesy of Launer Local History Room, Fullerton Public Library

"a lot of good people who had been longtime friends, Catholics and Protestants, . . . a lot of prejudice and feeling was triggered." But, he said, "It kind of dissipated over the years. The people settled down and forgot about it. The old friendships were renewed and I don't think people pay much attention to it anymore."

Hispanics

Hispanics drew interest mainly because of involvement in community controversy. The incidents opened the door for the opportunistic Klan, but more than Klansmen were involved. One case in point was the Santa Fe Railroad's 1919 proposal to build a concrete barracks at Highland and Santa Fe avenues to house its "Mexican employees." At a City Council meeting on January 21, 1919, a petition with signatures of 117 "prominent citizens" was presented protesting the action. Cocoltchos claimed in his dissertation that "The town's white population possessed uniformly negative images of the Hispanic population." The city protested to the railroad, and officials said they would change the site—if the city would pay certain expenses, including those for, "the work already done . . . amounting to about $8,000." That was refused, and the Santa Fe proceeded with construction despite a mass protest meeting on January 23, 1919, where, the *Tribune* reported, "they talked and talked and talked, but never got anywhere."

Nearly five years later, a similar incident involved the proposed location of a

"Mexican Colony" in unincorporated area south of Orangethorpe at Harvard Avenue (Lemon Street). A November 1923 *Daily Tribune* story headlined "Colony Plans Stalled by Purchase," reported that five ranchers on South Spadra (Harbor), "determined not to allow a Mexican colony to settle on the property adjoining their choice orange groves," had jointly purchased the ten-acre grove chosen as the site to house Hispanics being forced out of their homes in "Little Tia Juana . . . on the road between Fullerton and Anaheim."

In Louis Plummer's book on the history of Fullerton Union High School and Junior College, a story indicative of Hispanic-American relations of the period is related by Druzilla Mackey, a teacher in the school district's "Americanization" program. This educational program was initiated by the La Habra Citrus Association to teach its laborers about American ways, rules and regulations, extending even to instructions on how to buy their own homes. Miss Mackey said the program was organized in the summer of 1920 and found her moving into "La Habra Camp . . . sixty, three-room cabins on a breezy hillside" to live as one of the community.

In her interesting and poignant tale, Miss Mackey describes life in the camp and the success of the program, so much of the latter as to cause the high school district to expand it into other camps, including Fullerton, where the Placentia

The Fullerton area became well known for its citrus fruit products, particularly the valencia orange, but before oranges, walnuts were Fullerton's major exported agricultural crop. In one picture below we can see the packing crew of the local Diamond Walnuts plant where the sign boasts the company has "41 packing plants" and also proclaims that its walnuts have "more meat per pound." The second photo shows two wagons very heavily loaded—one might even say overloaded—with large bags of walnuts picked from Fullerton and area fields. Photos courtesy of Launer Local History Room, Fullerton Public Library

"Balboa Corporation to Become Important Factor in Fullerton's Industrial Activities," read a headline in the Fullerton Daily Tribune *in January 1924, and there were high hopes for the motor car manufacturer. The Balboa is depicted here in an ad. Illustration courtesy of Launer Local History Room, Fullerton Public Library*

The grading of Hillcrest Park—done by mule team—was a long and tedious task, but after more than a year of hard work a big celebration marked dedication ceremonies in May 1924, according to a series of stories in the Fullerton Tribune. *The park was once a motor court for travelers through the region and it served as a haven for victims of the 1933 Long Beach earthquake and of the floods of 1938. Photo by the author*

Orange Grower's Association had built twenty-four-four-room homes for its workers. Miss Mackey and others worked in this "model" colony—which, ironically, was occupied mostly by imported workers from Pomona and not the locals—as well as at seven separate colonies discovered on the Bastanchury Ranch. These colonies were made-up of "hovels" constructed of scrap sheet metal, discarded signs and fence posts. The largest of the colonies had thirty families "served by one lone water faucet and a few makeshift privies."

The program went well despite the obstacles, but after ten years of success, the Depression came and the accompanying "stress and strain" caused a change in attitude "The American community no longer spoke of 'our' Mexicans. They no longer considered that no 'whiteman' could pick oranges. Instead they felt that the jobs done so patiently by Mexicans for so many years should now be given to them. 'Those' Mexicans instead of 'our' Mexicans should 'all be shipped right back to Mexico where they belong,'" Miss Mackey wrote. Welfare representatives explained that jobs were no longer available to Hispanics and neither was welfare money—except for enough to furnish a free trip back to Mexico. "And so, one morning we saw nine train-loads of our dear friends roll away back to the windowless, dirt-floor homes we had taught them to despise." Of her work, Miss Mackey asked, "What were its lasting values? Quien Sabe."

But, this was also a period punctuated positively by significant actions which continue to have an impact on the daily lives of Fullerton's citizens. Among them are:

Zoning Laws. In a series of actions from March to May of 1923, Fullerton adopted its first zoning laws, designed to "create a city beautiful" by establishing "four distinct districts," as stories in the *Tribune* and *News* reported. There were two residential districts (apartments and single family homes) as well as manufacturing and business zones in the map prepared by "zoners" Fred West, W. J. Carmichael, and Robert Strain. There was only mild protest, and after slight modification the first zoning ordinance was adopted at the end of May 1923. Fourteen-plus years later, on October 21, 1947, a more extensive zoning ordinance was approved. According to a *Daily News-Tribune* story by Martin Bentson, the zoning law—Ordinance 524—"establishes zones in the city and regulates

the use of land, height of buildings, and yard spaces; adopts a map showing the boundaries of the zones; defines the terms used in the ordinance, provides for its adjustment, amendment, and enforcement; and prescribes penalties for violations."

Hillcrest Park. "The work of grading Hillcrest park is progressing steadily now, stated J. G. Seupelt, superintendent of parks, today," the *Daily Tribune* reported on April 30, 1923. "With the addition of three head of mules, the improvements have been given added impetus." Just over a year later—May 3, 1924, the *Tribune* reported on the dedication the park: "A big celebration marked the dedication of the City Park on Hillcrest this afternoon. The flag raising ceremony was executed by the Boy Scouts, who appeared dressed smartly in their Scout uniforms." Yvonne Irwin, attended by Mildred Walker and Esther Wilhite, made the flag presentation.

Other events of the period not only had an effect locally, but put Fullerton in the picture nationally, and even internationally. Among these were:

Boulder Dam Association. This group, formed to support the building of Boulder Dam, was organized in Fullerton on May 10, 1923, and it was here it had its headquarters as Representative Phil Swing, author of the Swing-Johnson Bill authorizing the project, rallied support for his cause.

Glenn Hartranft, Olympic Medalist. Glenn Hartranft, son of the S. C. Hartranfts, brought international attention to Fullerton in July 1924, when he won the silver medal in the shot put at the Olympic Games in France. The former star Fullerton Union High School athlete and Stanford student, nicknamed "Tiny," also came in sixth in the discus throw when he reportedly had an "off day."

Chapman for Vice President. The movement was serious; the Republican party wanted Charles C. Chapman to be the running mate of Calvin Coolidge in 1924. He debated with himself about the possibility before deciding against it, later writing, "While I am not insensitive to the high honor reflected on my being mentioned by friends, the press, and politicians for the second highest office in the Nation, I have since been profoundly thankful that I did not receive the nomination." This same year, Chapman was organizing director and board chairman of a new Los Angeles banking enterprise called Bank of America. That

Construction of a fountain in Hillcrest Park was enough reason to bring out a bevy of Fullerton's bathing beauties to test the water—although this was not an encouraged practice and it might well have been a chilly episode because this photo was among several taken on a December day in 1936. Photo courtesy of Launer Local History Room, Fullerton Public Library

More recently used as a recreation center, this building in Hillcrest Park, at Valley View and Lemon, was originally the American Legion Hall and was constructed in 1936. Photo courtesy of Launer Local History Room, Fullerton Public Library

William Hetebrink, Fullerton's street department foreman, was killed in this collision of a city dump truck and a Union Pacific Railroad "gasoline passenger car" at the South Harvard Avenue (Lemon Street) crossing on September, 16, 1925. Hetebrink, forty-eight, a passenger in the truck, was the first Fullerton city employee to die in an on-the-job accident and was the last of three Fullerton pioneer brothers, Fred and John having preceded him in death. Truck driver Sid Wilson was severely injured in the incident. A vehicular underpass at this location, constructed jointly by the city, county, and railroads, opened in May 1978. Photo courtesy of Launer Local History Room, Fullerton Public Library

bank, after a merger with the Commerce National Bank, was acquired by A. P. Giannini's Bank of Italy, which adopted the Bank of America name. (Giannini was a friend and business associate of Chapman and the latter served on the Bank of Italy board at one time)

Newspaper Editors Visit. Members of the National Editorial Association and spouses—567 persons strong in a parade of more than one hundred cars—came to the Charles C. Chapman Ranch in East Fullerton on June 29, 1926, as part of a county tour which followed a train trip from their San Diego convention site. Orange juice was served by eight Fullerton Union High School coeds and the visitors toured the groves, picking oranges from trees, before going to the California Hotel where they boarded "Parlor Cars" for a trip to Los Angeles.

Metropolitan Water District. Fullerton has been there right from the beginning. It was not one of the first nine communities to join the Metropolitan Water District of Southern California in 1928, but was among the next group of three and is considered one of the original thirteen cities comprising the district whose

Colorado River aqueduct has met Southland water needs for more than fifty years. Fullerton officially joined MWD on March 13, 1931, according to an early history, and Walter Humphreys was the city's first representative on the Board of Directors.

The decade of the 1930s produced events which would test the mettle of Fullerton's citizenry. Some did not survive—whole towns in the United States did not survive—but Fullerton did. In fact, in some instances the community prospered with capital improvements that stand as landmarks today. But it wasn't easy.

The Depression

"If it hadn't been for our good creditors we would have had to go into bankruptcy, but we battled it out and went through," is what Fred Strauss told his CSUF Oral History Program interviewer Esther Katz. He said, "We used to live on $15 a week," in a time when he would have lost his home if not for the "very lenient" Fullerton Building and Loan, which let him make interest-only payments of $8.88 a month.

When this writer discussed the era with historian and author Virginia Carpenter, she said, "It has always been my understanding that the people of this area sort of banded together and faced up to the situation. They survived without major problems, I've been told." That does not mean, however, that these were not troubling times here. Indeed, there was a toll taken on the community, indicated by the fact that many left the city. Fullerton's population declined during the decade by 418, a 3.8 percent drop from 10,860 in 1930 to 10,422 in 1940.

However, an example of just how well Fullerton did handle the Depression years is found in a statement issued by the Southern California office of the Work Projects Administration Division of Information. The WPA said, "A record of self-improvement considered unique in the United States has been made by Fullerton, California. . . . While other places moaned with depression-born financial headaches, this little city . . . built nearly $3,000,000 worth of public improvements and simultaneously reduced its public debt while holding down the tax rate . . . literally, the unemployment helped Fullerton and Fullerton helped itself and the unemployed."

Fullertonians took both usual—soup kitchens operated by the American

Efforts have begun to gather funds for the rebuilding of the fire-destroyed Izaak Walton Cabin in Hillcrest Park, home not only to the Conservation League but to Boy Scouts for many years. Photo courtesy of Launer Local History Room, Fullerton Public Library

A crowd gathered in July of 1924 for groundbreaking ceremonies for what was to become Chapman's Alician Court Theatre and is now known as the Fox Fullerton. Mrs. Alice Wilber Chapman turned the first shovel of direct as her husband C. Stanley Chapman (standing at right edge of main group) watched. Charles C. Chapman is the fifth man from the left. The Fullerton Daily Tribune *reported on May 29, 1925, that, "Throngs . . . blocked the courtyard of the beautiful Alician Court Theatre on North Spadra Road and completely filled the large auditorium for the performances at the opening." Inside, revelers were treated to many architectural delights, including, as the third picture (opposite page) shows, murals painted on the walls of the theater/auditorium. The building has also been known as the Mission Court Theater and the Universal Court Theater during its decades of service. Photos courtesy of Launer Local History Room, Fullerton Public Library*

Legion and by the schools—and some unusual steps to support each other, with a lot of the relief effort initiated by city government. City workers started the first local relief program by donating one day's pay each month to put the city's unemployed to work. This program started late in 1931, when, with the fund built up to $400-plus, four men were employed to work in the city parks at a salary of $4 a day. But the effort didn't end there. The city took full advantage of funding offered through the Reconstruction Finance Corporation, Civil Works Administration, State Emergency Relief Administration, Public Works Administration, and Work Projects Administration.

In a collection of "Historical Statistics," compiled by former librarian Carrie Sheppard in 1949, it is stated that the community actually, "made an investment in faith of its future of $5,614,000 in private and public funds," during its "ten depression years." John Newbauer, writing in an unpublished paper entitled, *An Epitome of The History of The City of Fullerton*, documented where many of the monies were spent, including the first buildings on the Fullerton College campus as well as Brea and Fullerton Creek flood control channel work. Newbauer credited Herman Hiltscher, city engineer and street superintendent of the era who later became Fullerton's first city administrator, with fostering "twenty-five projects . . . from the time he took charge of the Engineering Department until the City Hall was completed." He said, "Had it not been for Hiltscher's efforts these vital projects might have been tabled as the government geared itself for war." The WPA also credited Hiltscher, saying it was he, "to whom most of the leaders give a large share of credit for success of the program."

Hiltscher told the WPA that at one time as many as 850 workers earned their living on Fullerton relief projects and that the average over an eight-year period was around four hundred men. The native of Fullerton—whose father, August, was among Fullerton's first councilmen—discussed those times with a WPA represen-

tative while sitting in his office in the new City Hall, which, as fate would have it, was built on the site of the Hiltscher family home. "In fact," he told the WPA, "I was probably born within a few inches of the spot where I'm sitting right this minute." It was a remark that later made the soft-spoken, likeable administrator, the kidding target of barbs—by this writer, among others—about "not getting very far in life."

Among the more significant relief effort projects were several Work Projects Administration (WPA) projects that remain visible and viable today.

City Hall (Police Department). As noted before, most public building projects in Fullerton did not travel an easy course, and construction of Fullerton's first full-fledged City Hall

was no exception, even when federal funds became available. There was strong debate about location. Some still favored a site behind the Wilshire Avenue Fire Hall and others proposed building in Commonwealth Park (Amerige Park), a site actually approved by the City Council, which had plans prepared. Citizens, however, succeeded in getting an "initiative ordinance" placed on the ballot which barred building a City Hall in the park and, on December 8, 1936, voters approved it on a vote of 1,306 to 1,212.

You would recognize the City Hall plans prepared for the Amerige Park site, because it is the same building later constructed kitty-corner across the street at the northeast corner of Highland and Commonwealth (now housing the Police Department). That site was also the object of protest, many saying the price was too high, and others complained, "the distance . . . appeared to be too great for people to walk . . . to pay their water bill," according to Keith C. Terry's book,

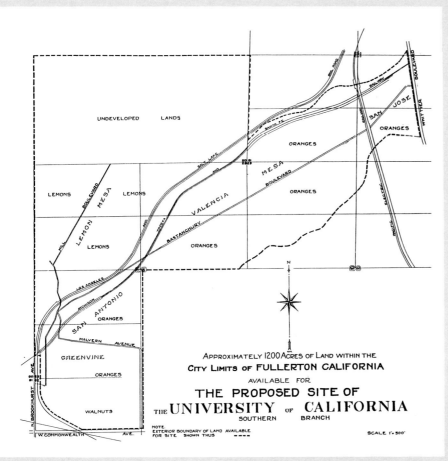

APPROXIMATELY 1200 ACRES OF LAND WITHIN THE
CITY LIMITS OF FULLERTON CALIFORNIA
AVAILABLE FOR
THE PROPOSED SITE OF
THE UNIVERSITY OF CALIFORNIA
SOUTHERN BRANCH

NOTE.
EXTERIOR BOUNDARY OF LAND AVAILABLE
FOR SITE SHOWN THUS -- -- --

SCALE 1"-500'

This map of the proposed Fullerton site for the southern branch of the University of California appeared in a booklet prepared by the Fullerton Chamber of Commerce in 1925. The "L"-shaped twelve hundred acres of land proposed for the site was made up mostly of Bastanchury Ranch lands. The parcel extended form Whittier Boulevard (Harbor Boulevard) at its extreme northeastern corner to Brookhurst and Commonwealth avenues at its extreme southwestern corner, an extension of Brookhurst Road serving as the western boundary. Map courtesy of Launer Local History Room, Fullerton Public Library

Walter M. Muckenthaler. Still other objections were based on the light-colored exterior of the proposed building, on grounds it, "would make it difficult for the baseball fans at Amerige Park, diagonally across Commonwealth, to see the games on Sunday afternoons," according to Warren Bowen, writing for the *Fullerton Observer* in August 1987. Bowen also said some, "objected to the 18 cents per $100 [assessed value] tax increase proposed."

The matter of walking distance was put to a test at a City Council meeting, Terry wrote, explaining that councilmen Muckenthaler and Tom Gowen led the fight for the Commonwealth/Highland site. When debate raged at one meeting, the men suggested "that august body take a hike to west Commonwealth and test the dispute. They did in short order." In the end, it was up to the people at a vote on August 15, 1939. Voters cast 1,640 *yes* votes and 920 *no* votes (adjusted to 1,711 to 929 when ballots were canvassed); Fullerton was finally going to have its own City Hall.

G. Stanley Wilson was architect for the Spanish-style building constructed by

Even as the university site was being proposed, Bastanchury Ranch was continuing to develop its agricultural resources. And, as the ranch was vast, so was the effort in preparing the former sheep grazing lands for cultivation, with the photo here attesting to the use of upwards of fifty mules at one time pulling five-or-six-mule team drags to flatten the land. By 1926, Gaston Bastanchury told the Fullerton News-Tribune he had already spent $600,000 on development and was prepared to spend between $300,000 and $400,000 more. The Bastanchury Ranch Company display at the 1925 Valencia Orange Show in Anaheim is seen at the top of the following page. Photos courtesy of Launer Local History Room, Fullerton Public Library

the "Federal Works Agency Work Projects Administration" under direction of H. Russell Amory, Southern California Administrator. Construction began September 28, 1939, the cornerstone—containing periodicals and statistical data of the day . . . and the arm bone of the old Indian found buried on the site— was laid on June 21, 1941, and the building was occupied at the start of 1942. Dedication ceremonies were held July 20 to 25, 1942, and the final words of the dedication program read: "This City Hall has been built to endure. It has been built to serve. It has been built to carry on civic enterprises in war and in peace." It has done all of that, serving as home to most city offices until 1963 and continuing today as the police headquarters building.

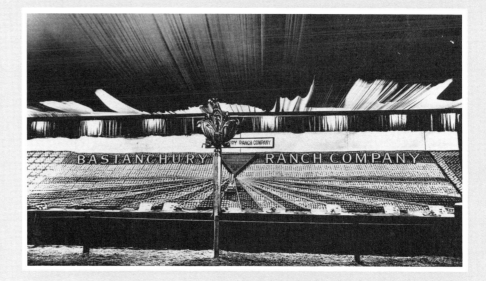

Post office (Commonwealth Station). It took less than seven months in 1939 for Fullerton and the federal government to conceive, plan and construct the first, and to this date only, federally owned building in Fullerton. The $56,000 Fullerton Post Office at the southeast corner of Pomona and Commonwealth

Avenues, now known as Commonwealth Station, was dedicated on Friday, October 27, 1939. Harrison Parkman, Post Office Department purchasing agent, "made the dedicatory address as personal representative of Postmaster General James A. Farley," the *Daily News-Tribune* reported. Parkman said postal service was established in Fullerton on March 4, 1888, with E. E. Beazley as postmaster, and that receipts for the first year "were approximately $300, of which Beazley's salary was $292.55." Now, fifty years later, postal receipts (for 1938) were between $45,000 and $50,000.

Library (Fullerton Museum Center). Two blocks north of the Post Office, another WPA project came to fruition with dedication ceremonies January 22-24, 1942, for the Fullerton Public Library building at the northwest corner of Pomona and Wilshire Avenues. Once again, it was a happy ending for a hard-fought campaign to provide adequate facilities. The Library built at that location in 1907 with the help of the Carnegie Foundation did not meet the needs of the growing community and several stopgap measures had been taken through the years, including building a cottage to house the children's section. The latter building later sold to the Girl Scouts and was moved to Hillcrest Park where it remains today after serving the Scouts and the American National Red Cross.

In September 1938, an application to the Public Works Administration for

As early as 1923 the Ebell Club, a Fullerton fixture since 1917, was looking into construction of a club building on two lots it had purchased in 1919 at the northeast corner of Harvard (Lemon) and Chapman avenues. However, it was not until 1924 that the building was constructed and dedication ceremonies were held on January 2, 1925. This was home to Ebell until it occupied its present clubhouse at 313 Laguna Road in 1962 and the property became part of the Fullerton College campus. Photo courtesy of Launer Local History Room, Fullerton Public Library

127

Fullerton's new Fire Station opened for service in August 1926, on the north side of the 100 block of West Wilshire, next to the alley behind the California Hotel. But it was more than a fire house, city offices being located on the upper floors where they shared space with the firefighters' "club rooms." Photo courtesy of Launer Local History Room, Fullerton Public Library

federal assistance in building a new library was rejected, but library trustees tried again, this time applying for a grant through the WPA, which was approved on June 6, 1940. Work on the building designed by Harry K. Vaughan began on September 12, 1940, and the structure was completed on Christmas Eve, 1941. Since 1973, when the library moved to its Commonwealth Avenue building, the Fullerton Museum Center, under auspices of the Fullerton Museum Association, has been housed under the building's distinctive red-tiled roof and behind its art-glass windows.

Fullerton College. The college had been housed since its inception in buildings on the Fullerton Union High School campus. As we know, some trustees felt the High School Auditorium money should have been spent on a separate junior college campus, and the availability of federal and state monies made this a much more obtainable goal. In its 1942 statement, the WPA said, "If Fullerton owes much to the unemployed, and vice versa, the same is even more true of the junior college. . . . Current financial report(s) of the institution . . . lists eight structures of the $2,382,410 plant built by WPA and PWA. Of these, PWA built an administration and social science building, commerce building and a locker room. WPA erected a shop building, stadium, ticket booth, technical trades building and pedestrian tunnels. The total cost of this including some general planning by WPA, amounted to $835,674."

Buildings were not the only Depression-era contribution to Fullerton public

These are the eight members of the Fullerton Police Department in 1927—including three who would serve as chief. In the picture, taken at the old police station behind the fire station on West Wilshire, are, back row, from left, Ernest Garner, S. R. Mills, Franke Moore, and R. C. Mills. In the front row, from left, are John Trezise, Chief James M. Pearson, John Gregory, and Jake Deist. Gregory and Garner also became chiefs of the Fullerton Department. Photo courtesy of Launer Local History Room, Fullerton Public Library

It was January of 1927 when a former sewer farm and pig ranch officially became an airport by action of the City Council, the site being leased to the Chamber of Commerce for five years at a fee of $1 per year. The first of these pictures was taken in the 1930s and the second shows the administration offices topped by the FAA control tower, the hub of activity at the eighty-acre facility. Photos courtesy of Launer Local History Room, Fullerton Public Library, and the author

works; there was also the matter of art, specifically murals painted as part of the Federal Works of Art Project. In a 1988 article about the murals, *Orange County Register* writer Laura J. Tuchman wrote, "In Freeway-riddled Orange county, Fullerton stands like a lone rose, a city whose urban ambiance lasts for more than a few blocks." Following are three examples of what she was writing about.

City Hall Mural. "The History of California," a three-panel mural in what was originally the council chambers of the new City Hall, was painted in 1942 by "post-surrealism" artist Helen Lundberg, under the auspices of the Work Projects Administration Federal Works of Art Project. The mural was covered over when the Police Department took over the building in 1963, and a lengthy restoration project costing more than $80,000 was completed in 1993.

Post Office Mural. The mural on the west interior wall of the lobby of the Commonwealth Station, depiction young people at work picking oranges in a grove, was painted by Illinois native Paul Julian. The work is perhaps, and unfortunately, best known for its inaccuracies, including depiction of a mostly Anglo crew, use of a step ladder rather than a straight ladder and the boxing of oranges in the field.

Fullerton High School Auditorium Mural. Charles Kassler was the artist for this Federal Works of Art Project, "a fresco of pastoral California," painted on the west exterior wall of the Fullerton High

School (Plummer) Auditorium. In Louis Plummer's history book, he quotes Los Angeles art critic Merle Armitage as saying, "Kassler has adhered not only to the beautiful traditions of pastoral California, but at the same time has also borne in mind the splendid Spanish architecture, and, lastly, created a beautiful fresco of amazing vitality and freshness of viewpoint." Some in the community did not

The International Order of Odd Fellows (I.O.O.F.) constructed this building in 1927. The building has for some time housed the Williams Company on its lower floor and at one time the Moose Lodge occupied the former Odd Fellows club rooms on the second floor. Photo courtesy of the author

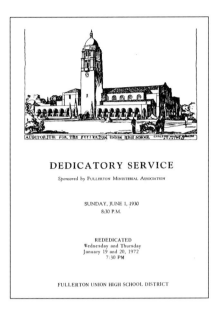

A most impressive addition to the Fullerton High School Campus, a structure which still today serves as a hub for cultural offerings, was dedicated in June 1930. The building was rededicated in December 1962 and again in 1972 after a refurbishing, as the Louis E. Plummer Auditorium. Reproduced here is a page from the original rededication program and a photo of the controversial murals—described as having "lurid colors and somewhat grotesque figures," in a 1939 newspaper article—which once adorned the west exterior wall of the building. Photos courtesy of the Launer Local History Room, Fullerton Public Library

agree, finding portions of the painting offensive, and in 1940 the fresco was painted out by order of the Board of Trustees.

But it was not only an economy in chaos, joblessness, and WPA projects that tested the spirit of Fullertonians in these times, they were also forced to pay their dues to Mother nature. First, it was a major earthquake and, five years later, residents battled a massive flood which claimed not only property, but lives.

The 1933 Earthquake

"The known death toll from Southern California's disastrous earthquake stood at 132 at noon today as a dozen towns and cities joined in a search for more bodies, caring for hundreds of injured and gauging property damage running into millions," read the United Press story in the March 11, 1933 editions of the *Fullerton Daily News-Tribune.* Long Beach counted 60 dead in the quake and series of "settling tremors" on the evening of March 10, and Santa Ana declared martial law "after a long night of terror in which buildings, rocked and riven, weaved in a dance of death," the newspaper reported.

"Fred Strauss was rouzed [*sic*] out of bed in the neighborhood of 4 a.m. today to be a hero for the refugees from Long Beach who were gathered around Hillcrest Park to escape a reported tidal wave. The American Legion had opened its hall to serve them breakfast and needed groceries, which Strauss provided," the paper reported. Sixty persons were served at the Legion Hall that first morning as Fullerton became a haven for refugees from Long Beach, Compton, Los Angeles, Bellflower and other cities. Many camped at Hillcrest Park, others accepted Charles C. Chapman's offer of five furnished apartments and many dozens more were taken into Fullerton homes. The city escaped without deaths, but damage was heavy and most of the city's schools required major rebuilding.

The 1938 Flood

Another disaster of nature literally swept through the city in the form of the largest flood on record. "Eight-foot Wall of Water Hits Atwood and Spreads Over Fullerton and Anaheim," a headline in the *Daily News-Tribune* read. The city actually took a double whammy, as, waters swept in from Atwood when the Santa Ana River surged over its west bank at about 3:00 a.m. on March 3, 1938, covering the south part of the city; and flood waters overflowed the Brea and Fullerton "barrancas" and "left a yawning gorge with vertical banks 20 or more feet deep through the heart of Fullerton."

Waters were contained within the barrancas by midday, but at the height of the surge, the swirling runoff—from a storm that deposited 2.90 inches of rain in twenty-four and 5.16 inches in thirty-six hours—played havoc. "At the east end of Brookdale Ave., a huge eucalyptus tree succumbed to the undermining of flood waters and heavy southerly winds, crashing across the flood to crush the back porch of the Lee Long home at 131 E. Brookdale," the newspaper reported. Water diverted by this obstruction carried parts of a duplex and a three-room house from Ellis Lane crashing down into the Spadra Road bridge, turning the structures "into kindling." Another harrowing tale involved Leslie Jondahl of Fullerton, who, while trying to help rescue a family near Yorba Linda, was swept off his feet by flood waters and "hurled down stream, tossed about like a cork," for a distance of three miles before coming to rest at a railway embankment in Atwood. Fullertonians weathered this challenge, too, only to once again brace themselves for the trials of war, this time in a bigger and more personal way than twenty-four years earlier.

World War II

"Typically, Fullerton set aside everything that was not essential to winning the war. Among other things, its citizens purchased in excess of $12,000,000 worth of bonds, and achieved the honor, during one of the bond campaigns, of being America's only 100 percent city, with every family in the city purchasing some form of war bond or stamps," Carrie Sheppard wrote in her "Historical Statistics" paper.

The Fullerton home for the Santa Fe Railroad since 1930, this station is listed on the National Register of Historic Places and is the centerpiece of Fullerton's Transportation Center and headquarters for AMTRAK. At this writing it is undergoing extensive refurbishing and remodeling by the Bushala Brothers under contract with the Fullerton Redevelopment Agency. Photos courtesy of Launer Local History Room, Fullerton Public Library, and the author

And so, Fullerton again centered its focus on a war effort, only this time it came closer to home. There were reports of Japanese submarines off the coast not more than twenty-five miles away; Fullerton Municipal Airport was closed to civilian traffic and both Army and Navy pilots used it for training; a lookout and radio communications center was established in the tower of City Hall; an air raid warning system was established and the city regularly practiced blackouts; and residents were concerned about spies.

In one instance, the latter concern proved genuine. The following story is related by Keith C. Terry in *Walter M. Muckenthaler*: "He lived in the small quarters off the garage and never bothered anyone. But the day after Pearl Harbor, Army offices came to the Muckenthaler home and arrested the Japanese gardener, much to the dismay of Walter and Adella (Muckenthaler). They learned over the next few weeks that their gardener had used his position . . . as a front for espionage work. When they searched his quarters, they found messages, newspapers and sophisticated cameras, all used in his work."

While giving their utmost at home, Fullerton's citizens also did not shy from their responsibilities away from it. In August 1943, the

The March 12, 1936 edition of Fullerton Junior College's Weekly Torch *newspaper contained a drawing of the Commerce Building, the first structure on the new campus, and the announcement that Bill Hay would be master of ceremonies for a cornerstone celebration that day. An article on the front page said buildings planned for the new campus, "will meet college needs for many years to come." It also said the School of Commerce Building depicted, "is planned to meet the needs of the school until 1950." In fact, the "Mexican-Californian type" two-story building of 70-by-150-foot dimensions is still serving the campus today. Illustrations courtesy of Launer Local History Room, Fullerton Public Library; photo by the author*

Fullerton Daily News-Tribune published a special "Honor Roll Edition," which listed the names of approximately thirteen hundred Fullerton men and thirty women then serving in the armed forces. The list included the names of two father-son teams in the U.S. Navy—Jess Koontz and son Donald and E. M. Parker and son Glenn—as well as Fullerton twins Beverly and Florence (better known as Jean and Joan) Cody, daughters of Mrs. Edith Cody, who were serving in the Womens Army Corps. The newspaper also told the story of the launching of a new escort

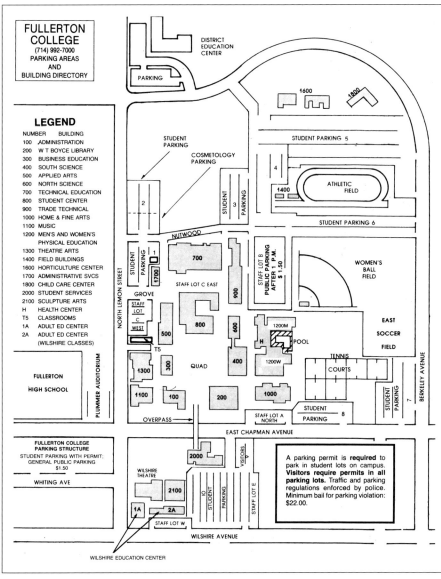

The campus of Fullerton College has expanded over the years to meet an ever increasing enrollment demand. Illustrated on the previous page is a map/directory of the campus as it appeared in the 1950s (including the Fullerton Union High School campus, both institutions then being under the same district administration) and, above, as it appears in 1993. You will particularly note in the early map that homes still line Harvard Avenue (Lemon Street) on the college side of the street. The Pacific Electric Railroad tracks cut through and formed the eastern edge of the college campus. Illustrations courtesy of Launer Local History Room, Fullerton Public Library

destroyer—the USS *Chambers*—which was named after Navy Ensign Russell Chambers of Fullerton, son of Mrs. R. L. Chambers and husband of Emma Ruth Chambers, who had been killed in the Philippines.

The final tribute to Fullerton's war contribution may be found in Hillcrest Park, where, at the Veterans Memorial, sponsored by the Fullerton Emblem Club, are listed the names of sixty Fullertonians who gave their lives in that great conflict.

The city mourned its losses, but took pride in its contributions, and in the aftermath of its sacrifice began to build—and build, and build. Carrie Sheppard's "Historical Statistics," provides figures indicating Fullerton's settlement into a growth pattern portending of still greater things. She wrote: "Postwar, Fullerton citizens again resumed their progressive activities with a renewed faith in the destiny of their city and during 1946 there was a total of $1,851,299.81 invested in homes and business properties. This trend continued through 1947, with a $1,892,563.35 total in building permits, and 1948 with $2,580,775.88 more. To date in 1949, this activity totals $2,326,624.40 in permits."

Among those statistics is included Fullerton's first large-scale tract development, the "Basque Tract" of 109 homes located north of Commonwealth Avenue along Basque Avenue developed by the Jewett Brothers, Richard and William, the same pair operating Fullerton Air Service. The tract's assessed valuation of $982,600 accounted for more than half of the 1947 building total.

This period in Fullerton history was brought to a high-soaring conclusion with a spotlight of world-record intensity focused directly on the community, specifically on two flight instructors at Fullerton Municipal Airport.

Flight of the Sunkist Lady

It was not only a high-soaring fete, it was a very, very long lasting one. Dick Riedel and Bill Barris took to the air from the Fullerton airport in a converted single-engined Aeronca airplane named the *Sunkist Lady* at 11:45 a.m. on March 15, 1949, and did not return to the ground until 11:47 a.m. on April 26, 1949. Riedel, Barris, and the *Sunkist Lady* had been aloft for a world record 1,008 hours and 2 minutes—42 days.

The record endurance flight was accomplished on the fourth try by Riedel and Barris, who secured the sponsorship of the Chamber of Commerce and received donations from all over the community. The pilots flew from Fullerton to Miami, Florida, and back, then circled Southland skies while logging more than 75,600 land miles and consuming 6,552 gallons of gasoline. It could not have been done without the support of the ground crew—Frank Miller, Don Janson, and Lloyd Colboch. They flew aboard a second Aeronca—the *Lady's Maid*—to airports along the flight route, where they would land, board Willys Jeepsters, and drive down the runway, passing up gasoline and food as the *Sunkist Lady* flew overhead.

Both men, after whom Fullerton streets have been named, went on to aviation careers, Riedel as chief pilot for Martin Aviation and Barris as chief pilot for Newt Bass, Apple Valley developer. They remained close friends until their deaths, within a month of each other, in 1974.

The symbol of Fullerton College, a blue and gold hornet sculpture, stands on the campus quad. The hornet has "buzzed" to fame through its students in many fields of endeavor, including athletic Hornets who have been honored as national champions in football and state champions in basketball and softball; musical Hornets who have won national Dixieland Jazz acclaim; entertainers who have become familiar names in American households; and one former student who resided in the White House (Pat Nixon). Photo by the author

Fullerton battled hard against the effects of the Depression, starting with city workers donating some of their salaries to put other people to work. The effort extended into the schools as well, where authorities made sure no one went hungry. Pictured here is the former Bastanchury Ranch School building, which was moved to the grounds of the Ford School and there, in 1934, was designed the "Ford School Soup Kitchen." Photo courtesy of Launer Local History Room, Fullerton Public Library

Amerige Park was the location for shooting of the film Alibi Ike, staring comedian Joe E. Brown. The film crew is seen here in March of 1935, all set to shoot a scene. Brown, holding a baseball bat on his shoulder, is standing at left center of the picture. Photo courtesy of Launer Local History Room, Fullerton Public Library

The Hotel Erle was a grand, three-story brick building at 115 West Commonwealth Avenue which later, starting in the 1930s, bore the name of Hotel Fullerton. The hotel was opened in July of 1924, according to a Fullerton Daily Tribune story, and this picture was probably taken close to that time. The building was demolished in the 1950s. Photo courtesy of Launer Local History Room, Fullerton Public Library

It was the month of the great flood in Fullerton—March 1938—but the game must go on. On March 31 at Amerige Park a photographer captured the action during a spring training exhibition game between Pittsburgh and Portland. Standing at first base (on the right) is Pirates star Paul Waner. Others in the photo are not identified. Over the left field fence you will note the stately McDermont/Gobar/Rich residence at 311 West Commonwealth Avenue, now the site of the main Fullerton Public Library. Photo courtesy of Launer Local History Room, Fullerton Public Library

The damage inflicted by raging flood waters is apparent in this picture taken March 3, 1938, at East Brookdale Place where Brea Creek flowed unchecked through the area. One house was swept away from this location, and, as is apparent, another sits precariously on the edge of the channel as does a garage on the other side. Photo courtesy of Launer Local History Room, Fullerton Public Library

When Fullerton Creek went over its banks, a good portion of the southeast section of the city was under water. Pictured here is South Spadra Road (Harbor Boulevard) at Southgate Avenue on March 3, 1938. Photo courtesy of Launer Local History Room, Fullerton Public Library

After viewing pictures of 1938 flood devasta-
tion, it's no wonder that public works projects
calling for concrete-lined flood control chan-
nels and check dams—with a lot of the money
coming through the federal Works Projects Administration—were rushed into production. Lin-
ing of Brea Creek was a priority, and these two
photos each looking easterly from the Basque
Avenue Bridge, show the difference it made.
The first photo was taken November 26, 1940,
as grading work was begun. The second photo
was taken February 3, 1941, as concrete walls
were being added to the concrete floor of the
channel. On the day of dedication, city officials
loaded into the backs of trucks and drove the
course of the channel and crowds cheered from
above. Photos courtesy of Launer Local History
Room, Fullerton Public Library

Integral to flood control was construction of two dams in Fullerton, one being the Brea Dam, located just east of Harbor Boulevard near the North
Orange County YMCA. The first picture here is a view of the site taken on July 12, 1940, and looks northwesterly. The second photo, also looking
northwesterly, was taken in 1942 (date unspecified) and shows the major portion of the dam completed. Photos courtesy of Launer Local History Room,
Fullerton Public Library

While construction was proceeding on the Brea Dam, the same thing was happening on the east side of the city where Fullerton Dam is located just west of Associated Road. Here we first see the site in a southeasterly view taken on July 26, 1940; then the upstream side of the dam looking toward the west, photographed on October 24, 1940. Note the oil derricks in the background. Photos courtesy of Launer Local History Room, Fullerton Public Library

Herman A. Hiltscher is given a great deal of credit for Fullerton's successful capital improvement projects during the Depression years and beyond. Hiltscher was city engineer during the 1930s and, when a separate city administrative branch of government was created in 1953, he became the city's first city administrator. He brought on Robert Clark to lead the city's industrial development effort, and the result was $2.5 million worth of new industry in three years. Photo courtesy of Launer Local History Room, Fullerton Public Library

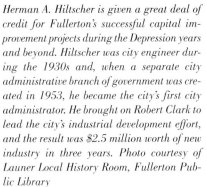

After extended controversy about the site, ground was broken at the northeast corner of Highland and Commonwealth avenues for a City Hall. The site, seen here in a 1939 photo when still occupied by the home where Herman Hiltscher, Fullerton's first city administrator, was born, was later owned by Adam Brandle, local hotel owner, who sold it to the city. Construction was completed December 24, 1941, and the building was occupied the first week in January 1942. John Raitt, FUHS grad who went on to Broadway fame, offered vocal numbers at dedication ceremonies July 25, 1942, and the program notes concluded: "This City Hall has been built to endure. It has been built to serve. It has been built to carry on civic enterprises in war and in peace." At left, City Hall is seen soon after its completion. Photos courtesy of Launer Local History Room, Fullerton Public Library

The famed murals which adorn the council chambers of the new City Hall are seen here in a photo of the 1948 City Council in session. The dedication program in 1942 took special note of the "soft, rich tones of the murals, designed by Miss Helen Lundberg and Miss Miriam Farrington of the Works Progress Administration Art Department." Seated at the council table in this 1948 photo are, from left, Tom Eadington, councilman; Herman Hiltscher, city engineer; Vern Wilkinson, councilman; Irvin Chapman, mayor; Carrie Adams, city clerk; Homer Bemis, councilman; C. R. Allen, city attorney; and Hugh Warden, councilman. Photo courtesy of Launer Local History Room, Fullerton Public Library

The Fullerton Police Department has been headquartered in the Commonwealth and Highland facility since it was built, but after the new City Hall was completed across the street in 1963, the department took sole possession of the structure. An annex to the building, visible in this picture, was constructed north of the original City Hall along Highland Avenue. The facilities have been named in honor of the late Wayne H. Bornhoft, police chief when the department took over the building and built the annex and who, after retirement, became mayor of Fullerton. Photo by the author

Fullerton's Post Office was another WPA project that still serves the public today. The building is now known as the Commonwealth Station. The interior Post Office photo (next page) shows C. C. Clark, later postmaster, and Henry Dyckman tending the clerk's windows. The mural on the west interior wall of the Commonwealth Station lobby (next page) was painted by Illinois native Paul Julian. Photos courtesy of Launer Local History Room, and the author

Facing page: Bill Barris and Dick Riedel put Fullerton on the national map in 1949—and they did it by staying off city turf for forty-two days. Between March 15 and April 26 the two pilots stayed aloft in their single-engine airplane, flying first to Florida, then returning and circling over the area until they had set the world's airborne endurance record. They are seen here on board their airplane before taking off and again as they received supplies from a Jeepster racing along the runway as they flew slowly overhead. They were welcomed home in a grand parade down Commonwealth Avenue and up Spadra Road (Harbor Boulevard). Photos courtesy of Launer Local History Room, Fullerton Public Library

CHAPTER IX

Giant Strides

1950–1970

Fullerton opened this era with a population of 13,958, but "times, they were a-changin'." This historical period will be remembered as one of transition, during which the community embarked on a journey of transformation, taking giant strides in growth, in establishment of a more diversified economic base, in expanded cultural and academic horizons, and in major civic improvements. And, all was done in accordance with a brand new Master Plan whose basic tenets still guide the city today.

Growth? Indeed—It was so fast and so furious that city officials began estimating the population between censuses in order to gain much needed state tax-sharing revenue. The numbers look like this: 1952–19,050, 1953–22,779, 1954–27,546, 1955–36,016—an increase since 1950 of 22,058 or 158 percent in five years. By 1960 the U.S. Census set the number at 56,180, an increase of 42,222 in the decade—302 percent—and by 1970, Fullerton's population was 85,987, a 20-year increase of 72,029—516 percent. This spells growth, as in capital G-R-O-W-T-H.

Population growth is one thing, but its accompanying activities are something else unto themselves. We are talking major milestones about which pages and pages could be written. We are looking at the advent of freeways; at introduction of California State University into the academic and cultural mix; at library expansion, a new City Hall; and at a local "industrial revolution" which provided a new economic base. This progressive package is reflected in another interesting set of numbers, namely the measure of the city's value. At the start of this historical period Fullerton had an assessed valuation of $32,144,410, which represented about a $12 million increase, or 60 percent, over the preceding thirty years. By 1960, the assessed valuation was $111,281,250—an increase of $79.1 million or 246 percent, in ten years—and in 1970 it had reached $267,914,212—an increase of $235.8 million, or 734.6 percent in twenty years. This increasing tax base enabled the city to actually lower the tax rate, from $1.37 cents per $100 of assessed valuation in 1950–1951 to $1.29 per $100 in 1970–1971. The tax rate had been as high as $1.685 in 1951–1952 (The all-time high was $2 per $100 during the height of the Depression in 1932) and had been steadily reduced.

This aerial photo of downtown Fullerton, taken July 14, 1953, looks straight north up Spadra Road (Harbor Boulevard). At the bottom of the photo note that there is still a railroad grade crossing on Spadra, the underpass not being constructed until 1970. Near the top of the picture, the Pacific Electric viaduct over Spadra Road is still in place. Some of the landmark structures are seen as they appeared forty years ago, such as the Chapman Building (center of photo, with the "Famous" sign painted on it) and the Masonic Temple, the Fox Fullerton Theater, and the Amerige Block. Photo courtesy of Launer Local History Room, Fullerton Public Library

But, where does one start describing this phenomenon? Perhaps a logical choice is planning, for without it any pattern of growth surely could not have been sustained. An article about Fullerton in the April 1956 edition of *Architectural Forum* magazine said, "Probably the best way to avoid the problems of renewing a city is to assure well-planned development in the first place . . . the city of Fullerton, Calif., forms a case study of one young city's efforts to avoid the growing pains of fast, haphazard development and their delayed after-effects of deterioration and blight."

The article said "careful thinking and acting from 1940 on," by the city's

A demonstration in the rapid building of a tract home put on by the Jewett Brothers Construction Company at the Lions Club's Fullerton Community Fair in May 1950, typified the rapidly expanding Fullerton of the 1950s. The Jewetts, Richard and William, and their crew constructed their "Clipper" home in fifty-seven hours and fifty-seven minutes. A telegram from the National Association of Home Builders in Washington, D.C., congratulated the firm on their record-breaking accomplishment which "clearly disproves propaganda disseminated from many places—particularly, Washington, D.C—that the home building industry has not kept pace in modern construction techniques and efficiencies." Photos courtesy of Launer Local History Room, Fullerton Public Library.

stewards were responsible for Fullerton avoiding the decay experienced by many communities. The magazine reported that from 1952 to 1956, "Plans and enterprises put into construction . . . created 4,100 new jobs with another 7,150 . . . in prospect . . . in about another year." The magazine specifically cited adoption of a zoning map, vigorous subdivision requirements and formation of an industrial development program as prime examples of "careful thinking and acting."

With all of this happening, and even as effective as the zoning laws had been in guiding this growth, it was apparent Fullerton needed more. It came in the form of a Master Plan for community development.

Master Plan

In a report to the Fullerton City Council in July 1958, the Planning Commission announced, "For the first time in its history, Fullerton has an adopted, official and complete Master Plan. Following long and at times bitterly contested Public Hearings, Elements 1 and 2 were adopted on June 4, 1957, followed by the remaining three elements exactly one year later, on June 4, 1958." The report, submitted by Planning Commission Chairman Ralph McLean and produced principally by Planning Director and Commission Secretary Don DeWitt, called the plan "a good one," although, "not one that is now and will forever be perfect." The later prediction proved sound, as attested to by the many amendments that have followed, but the plan's basic elements have consistently guided the city through its most turbulent times.

Fullerton residents were to see many development plans—from civic center, to Brea Dam basin recreation area, to traffic planning, to downtown redevelopment—submitted under this Master Plan, but another, important element of Fullerton growth had already begun in the form of an economic base already in transition.

Industrial Development

At the start of this period, Fullerton was still receiving 40 percent of its revenue from oil, but the num-

The city's fiftieth anniversary of incorporation also provided an opportunity for former Olinda or Fullerton High teammates of Hall of Famer Walter "Big Train" Johnson to gather and reminisce. From left are Hollis Knowlton, Robert McFadden, Charles Hansen, George Kammerer, Cob Isbell, Fayette Lewis, John Tuffree, and Joe Wagner. Photo courtesy of Launer Local History Room, Fullerton Public Library

bers were starting to slip even as the city's population and concurrent demands for services grew. The city obviously had—or soon would have—a revenue dependency weakness. Community leaders took action to rectify the situation, producing an industrial development program that fit in with ongoing planning efforts.

The *Architectural Forum* article, reprinted in the *Fullerton News-Tribune* in April 1956, gives us insight into how this was done. The magazine described one of the city's "wisest moves" as the 1952 hiring of Robert B. Clark to lead the industrial development program. Clark's plan was simple: (1) Get more land for industry; (2) Develop a comprehensive growth program; (3) Attract new industry. The city took care of (1) and (2) through the Master Plan and Clark took care of (3), enticing such firms as Kimberly-Clark and Sylvania Electric Products, among others, to locate large industrial facilities in Fullerton's newly designated industrial parks.

The first underpass built in Fullerton was opened to service in April 1960 at the former grade crossing of Nicolas Avenue (Euclid Street). The first photo, looking to the southwest, shows the grade crossing in August 1957. The second photo provides a clear view of the underpass with the bridge nearly complete. Photos courtesy of Launer Local History Room, Fullerton Public Library

Kimberly-Clark Corporation's huge plant in East Fullerton was in the vanguard of Fullerton's big industrial development program. Kimberly-Clark's first Fullerton-produced Kleenex tissues rolled out on April 16, 1956, and by the time the facility was into its tenth year its work force had increased from 170 to 534, the 738 freight cars of finished products had climbed to 2,975 carloads and the two products produced the first year had grown to a full line of consumer goods. Photo courtesy of Launer Local History Room, Fullerton Public Library

The firm that very rapidly became Fullerton's largest employer—and remains so today—came on the scene in 1957, clearing land off a hilltop at the northeast corner of Gilbert and Malvern avenues and building the facility now easily recognized as Hughes Aircraft Company. This aerial photo, taken in 1964, shows the administration and engineering buildings on the site. Employment at Hughes in Fullerton peaked at about fifteen thousand in the 1980s, diminished with defense cutbacks in the early 1990s but still leads Fullerton employment rolls with more than seven thousand at this writing. Photo courtesy of Launer Local History Room, Fullerton Public Library

Freeways

On the state level it began in 1947 with authorization to use gas tax monies for highway construction. Locally, it began at Fullerton's southwestern border with building of the Santa Ana Freeway, specifically with opening of a 1.25-mile link through Buena Park from Fullerton Creek (near Artesia Avenue) to Orangethorpe Avenue on the morning of July 3, 1957. In September 1958, a section of the Riverside Freeway between Spadra (Harbor) and Magnolia Avenue was opened. Fourteen months later (November 18, 1959), a 2.7-mile section between Spadra and Cypress Street (State College Boulevard) completing the freeway between Magnolia Avenue in Fullerton and the City of Riverside.

Fullerton freeway building concluded at the eastern edge of the city with the Orange Freeway (Route No. 57) which opened to traffic in stages over a three-year period, i.e., the Riverside Freeway to Nutwood link in the summer of 1969, Nutwood to Imperial (2.3 miles) in June of 1970, and Imperial to the Pomona Freeway (4.7 miles) in 1972.

Underpasses

Transportation-oriented construction was not limited to the city's borders. Infrastructure projects were highlighted by advent of underpasses providing railroad grade separations

144

at key locations. The first underpass, built at a cost of $800,000, was the Nicolas (Euclid) Underpass which opened April 18, 1960. The Commonwealth Underpass ($1.3 million) was next, being dedicated June 1, 1962; then the Harbor Underpass ($2.5 million), October 1970; the Lemon Underpass ($4.3 million), May 1978; and, the most recent, the Gilbert Underpass ($6 million) in February 1987.

The themes of this era are giant strides forward and transformation, but Fullerton's people could not escape the effects of battles in faraway lands.

Effects of War

Twice in this era war was visited upon our nation and once again the community paid a price. First it was the Korean War of 1950–1953, and then the 1960s most predominant historical event, the Vietnam War, which extended into the mid-1970s. The latter raised emotional hackles like none before it, and even as debate was carried on along the city's streets and on its campuses, the community once again did its part in support of its nation. In the end, however,

The Hunt Branch Library (upper right) was a $500,000 gift to the city from Hunt Foods and Industries Foundation in 1962. The project was carried out in a coordinated efforts between Hunts and the city, which found the company expanding facilities while the city was building the $1.3 million Commonwealth Underpass (seen here at left). Photo courtesy of Launer Local History Room, Fullerton Public Library

It wasn't until the late 1950s that Nicolas Avenue (Euclid Street) was extended northerly beyond Valencia Mesa Drive. The first photo, looking south toward Valencia Mesa, shows the dirt road that extended into the former Bastanchury Ranch properties. The second photo (facing page, top) is a similar view of the area in about 1961, after completion of a project extending the street from Valencia Mesa to Imperial Highway. Photos courtesy of Launer Local History Room, Fullerton Public Library

comes the realization that battles fought over ideals and principals inevitably take their highest toll in the most personal way, in the lives of a nation's young people. The Veteran's Memorial at Hillcrest Park tells us that forty-seven of Fullerton's potential leaders died on the battlefields of these two conflicts, seventeen in Korea and thirty in Southeast Asia.

As faraway battles took a heavy toll here, an institution having a most profound impact on the community, even extending to future's infinity, came to Fullerton in the form of an addition to the "Groves of Academe," as the *Orange County Register*'s *LEGACY: The Orange County Story* had so labeled the city.

California State University, Fullerton

As difficult as it was to swallow rejection of Fullerton as a university site in 1924, it was easy to understand the joy and anticipation that swept the community in the late 1950s when it was learned the city would host a state college campus. Establishment of the college was authorized by the California legislature in 1957 (Senate Bill 2680 appropriated $1.65 million for the facility and Chapter 1681 of the California Statutes of 1957 officially established the school), but the local celebration did not begun until November 1958, when the California Public Works Board officially designated the site as being in East Fullerton at Cypress Street (State College Boulevard) and Pioneer Avenue (Yorba Linda Boulevard). The original 235-acre site was purchased in 1959 (a contiguous 17-acre parcel was added later).

What was originally called Orange County State College—with 452 full and part-time students and 46 employees (including 24 part-time faculty)—held its first classes in the fall of 1959 in temporary quarters at Sunny Hills High School. The administration, headed by Dr. William B. Langsdorf as president, had offices at Fullerton High School in the original Fullerton College building. The Titans—the nickname selected by election of the student body that first year—were on their way.

In 1960 the college moved to its campus, housed there in temporary buildings even as construction began on the first permanent structure, the Letters and Science Building (McCarthy Hall), which opened in 1963. The Music Building opened in 1964, the Physical Education Building in 1965, and construction on the campus has continued, with several major projects now in progress. The college underwent its first name change in 1962—the first of five in the school's first fifteen years—when it became Orange State College. Other names: California State College at Fullerton (July 1964); California State College, Fullerton (July 1968); and, finally California State University, Fullerton (June 1972).

The school's nickname and its symbol, the elephant, came together in a spectacular campus attraction that captured international attention on May 11, 1962—an elephant race. A fictitious Elephant Racing Club, born as a class project, became a reality when other institutions of higher learning, including Yale and Harvard, took up the challenge and began acquiring elephants for the big race. The event was held near the northwest corner of the campus—an area quickly dubbed "Dumbo Downs"—and, much to the shock of Fullerton police and Elephant Racing Club members, more than ten thousand spectators turned out to watch the proceedings which featured a runaway elephant that scattered the crowd surrounding the open field.

Some have said that was the start of the school's sports tradition, but in a more traditional sense it began when Coach Alex Omalev's 1961–62 basketball team, led by Edgar Clark and Leonard Guinn, gained national recognition by advancing to the quarterfinals of the National Association of Intercollegiate Athletics (NAIA) basketball tournament. That winning tradition has continued with national championships in baseball, softball, gymnastics, women's basket-

All of North Orange County was involved in building St. Jude Hospital, which opened its doors to patients in May 1957, under the operational direction of the Sisters of St. Joseph of Orange. Public subscription drives were held in the communities the hospital was designed to serve and, when the 125-bed hospital opened its doors, it was expected the facility would be sufficient for many years to come. But within three days the facility was filled to capacity and ten years later—1967— the hospital turned away some 1,653 patients for lack of bed space. This prompted the facility's first of several expansions and advances, a $5.3 million project in 1968–1969 which included an 80-bed rehabilitation center and brought about a name change—St. Jude Hospital and Rehabilitation Center— that more appropriately described the facility. Now, it is St. Jude Medical Center, a name that properly describes the full spectrum of medical services available to this area's residents. Photo by the author

ball, cross-country and women's fencing (in 1979, CSUF was the only school in the nation with two top-division national champions, baseball and women's gymnastics) and through the names of former CSUF athletes playing at the major league level in football, basketball, and baseball.

CSUF's first decade was not all building and accomplishment, nor all the "fun and games" of elephant races. The late 1960s brought controversy to the campus, first through student production in 1967 of the play, *The Beard*, which found many in the com-

In 1982, officialdom of the Orange Diocese of the Catholic Church visited St. Jude Hospital and Rehabilitation Center on the occasion of its twenty-fifth anniversary. From left are Monsignor Joseph Pekarick, Bishop William Johnson, and the Reverend Joseph Smith, longtime chaplain at the hospital. Photo courtesy of Launer Local History Room, Fullerton Public Library

This view of what was to become the California State University, Fullerton campus, was taken May 4, 1960, just as construction began on temporary classroom (upper right). The road running across the bottom of the photo is Pioneer Avenue (Yorba Linda Boulevard) and the perpendicular road running at the bottom (center, bottom) is Associated Road. The orange groves at the bottom portion of the picture are now taken up by the Fullerton Arboretum, the Titan Sports Complex, and parking lots. Nine different landowners were involved when the state purchased the 225 acres making up the campus. Photo courtesy of Launer Local History Room, Fullerton Public Library

munity objecting to the language and sexually explicit scenes, and, in 1969–1970 through demonstrations centering on a draft/Vietnam War protest, which brought the police SWAT squad to the campus.

The true measure of such incidents, however, rests in their resolution. These incidents have seemed, in the long run, to cement a positive relationship between community and university. As graduates—more than one hundred thousand of them through 1993—have been absorbed into the community and community representatives have become involved in school planning and activities, co-operation has been the theme and constructive growth the result. This relationship is epitomized by the unique joint powers agreement between university and city that has brought to reality the Mariott Hotel Conference Center and Titan Sports Complex

It is a grown-up but still building university—offering ninety-one degree programs (forty-four of them at the graduate level) in seven schools of instruction to nearly twenty-five thousand students—which graces the 252-acre campus today. Five persons have served in the office of president—William B. Langsdorf (1959–1970), L. Donald Shields (1971–1980); Miles D. McCarthy (acting, 1980), Jewel Plummer Cobb (1980–1990), Milton A. Gordon (1990–)—and guided the university's growth through its first one-third of a century.

The school has played host to Ronald Reagan as both governor (1970) and president (1988); alumnus Kevin Costner came "home" (1992) to open the sports

Thirty-two years after the previous photo, this is an aerial view of the northwest corner of the California State University, Fullerton campus, showing the Titan Sports Complex opened in the spring of 1992. Left, foreground, is the baseball field with the main softball field beyond it. Right, foreground, is the multipurpose Titan Stadium (occupied here for the first time at commencement exercises in May 1992) and beyond that the eight-lane all-weather track and soccer practice field, tennis courts, and practice fields. Campus buildings can be seen in the background. Photo by Pat O'Donnell, courtesy of CSUF Public Affairs Office.

This aerial photo of Cal State Fullerton taken in April of 1963 shows construction well under way on the first permanent campus structures, featuring the letters and science building (now McCarthy Hall). The first home of the future two-time national champion baseball team is clearly visible in the photo. Photo courtesy of Launer Local History Room, Fullerton Public Library

Cal State Fullerton athletics, some say, began with the elephant races held even before there were buildings on the State College Boulevard campus. In a more traditional sense, the 1961–1962 CSUF (then known as Orange County State College) basketball team coached by Alex Omalev put Fullerton on the map by advancing to the quarterfinals of the National Association of Intercollege Athletics (small college) tournament. Edgar (Bean) Clark, a leader on that team, is pictured scoring against the University of Redlands. Photo courtesy of Edgar Clark

complex; the Titan gymnasium was home to team handball in the 1984 Olympic Games; the school became a regional site (1988) for the California Humanities Project; the school's Gerontology Center (1988) was built solely with contributed funds; the El Dorado Ranch in central Fullerton was given (1989) the university for use as the president's home; Heritage House, a restored 1894 Fullerton home, opened (1976) in a new setting in the campus Arboretum; and CSUF has spread its wings with the opening (1989) of a branch campus in Mission Viejo.

As the university was cutting through uncharted Fullerton waters, another, more familiar, civic endeavor was being launched. The city was again in need of administrative office space, and this time, in keeping with Master Plan objectives, it would be more than just a building; this time plans were made for a complete Civic Center.

Fullerton Civic Center

A civic center complex—City Hall, Library, Police Department—stands today on its West Commonwealth Avenue location after rejection of much more elaborate proposals for development. The Los Angeles architectural firm of Smith Powell and Morgridge, in June 1959, submitted detailed plans for Civic Center developments on two sites to Fullerton officials. One location was twenty-seven acres on the west side of Spadra Road (Harbor Boulevard) across from Hillcrest Park, now occupied by a shopping center and the North Orange County Court facilities. That plan envisioned construction of a major highway along the Pacific Electric right-of-way (now Berkeley Avenue) and a magnificent auditorium fronted by a two-story waterfall and reflecting pool. The other plan encom-

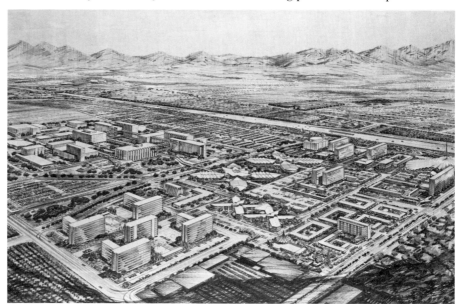

Even as plans progressed for Fullerton's new university campus, private developers unveiled an ambitious plan for development around the university. The campus is seen at left center in this architect's rendering of plans for development submitted by College Park Fullerton. The $75 million plan featured "a bold new concept in the building of a total college-oriented community . . ." with hotels, apartments, commercial space, and recreation areas and was highlighted by a proposal to take Commonwealth Avenue underground north of Chapman Avenue and bring it up to grade again at Nutwood. Commercial structures were to be built over the top, and the plan also called for a ski-jumping and ice-skating rink (center, right in rendering) and a hotel complex and a high-rise apartment district off of State College (lower left). As you can see, several portions of the plan became reality before the College Park Fullerton group broke up and land was sold off to individual developers. Photo courtesy of Launer Local History Room, Fullerton Public Library

passed twenty acres on both sides of a widened Highland Avenue between Commonwealth and Whiting avenues, which also included an auditorium and a proposal to make Highland a major thoroughfare through the city (supplanting Spadra) by connecting it to Spadra at Union Avenue and building an underpass at the railroad tracks.

The plans were magnificent—and they were expensive, too expensive. Working with the architects, the city decided on a more conservative course by modifying the Highland/Commonwealth plan. The new City Hall would be built as designed at the northwest corner of the intersection, but reoriented to face Commonwealth rather than Highland. This did away with the grandiose Highland thoroughfare proposal, and its attendant auditorium and art gallery and museum, while leaving intact the plan to convert the old City Hall to police facilities.

The City Hall, built at a cost of $1,977,085, contains forty-eight thousand square feet of space in its three stories and basement. It has housed city administrative offices, other than police and fire, since its dedication on June 1, 1963. But, once again, a public construction project did not come easy. On September 6, 1962, at about 8:30 a.m., construction workers were pouring cement for the third floor at the east end of the building when steel supports apparently failed and the whole section collapsed, spilling tons of wet cement and steel onto the second floor. Eleven workmen were injured in the incident, four of them being hospitalized temporarily.

Civic improvements did not stop there. Fullerton has been studying expansion of library services for a decade, and in the 1960s great strides were taken in that area, including a branch library and locating a site for a new main library in keeping with the Civic Center concept.

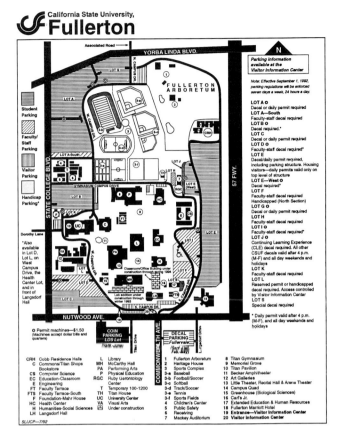

This map of the campus at Cal State Fullerton shows buildings completed and under construction as classes began for the fall semester of 1992. Map courtesy of Public Affairs Office, California State University, Fullerton

Fullerton's City Hall is seen under construction at the bottom of this aerial photo which was probably taken in early 1963. The photo, looking north up Highland Avenue also provides a view of the former Ford School (left, just below center), which was built in 1920 and razed in 1963 to make way for "The Fountains" housing development. Also seen is the El Dorado Ranch (just above center) then owned and occupied by C. Stanley Chapman and now the residence of the president of California State University, Fullerton, and, while land has been cleared just beyond the ranch, there is, as yet, no North Orange County Municipal Court nor shopping mall across from Hillcrest Park (right, just above center). Photo courtesy of Launer Local History Room, Fullerton Public Library

Fullerton's new and former City Halls are seen in this photo taken soon after the new facility was opened in 1963. Photo courtesy of Launer Local History Room, Fullerton Public Library

Branch Library

The Hunt Branch Library, Fullerton's first such facility, constructed largely with funds donated by Norton Simon and the Hunt Foods and Industries Foundation, was opened in the west end of the city. The 10,000-square-foot facility, designed to accommodate thirty-five thousand volumes and opening with fifteen thousand volumes in its stacks, was dedicated on September 12, 1962. The ceremonies were attended by Simon, who presented a deed to the property to the city, part of a Foundation gift totaling $485,000, which also covered full costs of design and construction and part of the cost for landscaping and furnishings.

Library planning was not confined to the branch facility, because, since the start of the decade, Library Trustees had been concerned about adequacy of the Main Library. In 1967, Margaret Ward, a state library consultant, recommended steps be taken toward construction of a new facility and cited Fullerton "as a city which needs above-average library service to meet the demands of a population which is superior in education, employment level and cultural interests." Another study that year by the League of Women Voters also concluded the Main Library was inadequate and, in 1969, the Library Board of Trustees, working with professional library staff and consultants, recommended a new facility on a new site—adjacent to the new City Hall.

Thus, as the city prepared to enter a new decade and a new era, an institution that had been with the community since almost the very beginning—a library— was again on everyone's mind. Construction of a new Main Library was a million dollar decision that would face Fullerton voters just months into this new historical period.

Fullerton city officials are pictured in 1963 in the Council Chambers of the new City Hall. Seated at the council bench, from left, are Stanley B. Christensen, city attorney; Everette Farnsworth, councilman; Burton Herbst, mayor; Howard Cornwell, councilman; Duane Winters, councilman; and Herman Hiltscher, city administrator. At the staff desk, center front, is Virginia Fitzsimmons, city clerk. In the foreground at the press desk, back to camera, is the author. Photo courtesy of Launer Local History Room, Fullerton Public Library

For forty years the main Fullerton fire station was the two-story structure at 123 West Wilshire Avenue, but, in 1966, the department moved into the sparkling new facilities at 312 East Commonwealth Avenue. The new headquarters station was funded via a bond issue approved by voters in 1962 which also provided money for Station No. 5 and Station No. 6. Photo courtesy of Launer Local History Room, Fullerton Public Library

In 1994 Fullerton will celebrate the thirtieth anniversary of one of its most successful community events, the "Night in Fullerton" celebration of the community's cultural attractions. Night in Fullerton was created by the Fullerton Arts Committee of the Chamber of Commerce under direction of Dr. Edward Struve and William McGarvey, Jr., in 1964, the first event being held October 23 of that year with Dorian Hunter as chairperson. There were between 4,000 and 5,000 visitors to six locations during that first celebration; in 1992 the crowd numbered between 25,000 and 30,000 visitors at fourteen sites. "What it is meant to do is give people a taste of what goes on during the year," Fullerton Museum Center Director Joe Felz said in 1992 of the event which is now held in the spring of the year. This photo of the Fullerton College Jazz Band performing in the courtyard of Villa del Sol was taken in 1984. Another featured community celebration is the Founders Day Parade and Street Faire marking the city's 1887 founding which is held in early May of each year. In year's past, the Fourth of July was occasion for a huge celebration, a tradition renewed with the Fireworks Show and Festival held at Fullerton Union High School Stadium. Photo courtesy of Launer Local History Room, Fullerton Public Library

The Union Pacific Railroad was the last of
the three railways serving Fullerton to arrive—the Santa Fe and Pacific Electric (later
Southern Pacific) preceding it. The UP completed building its depot in 1923, a distinctive building with a mission tile roof, cupola,
and octagonal dome. The depot was purchased by the city's redevelopment agency in
1980, moved across Habor and became the
Spaghetti Factory. Photos courtesy of Launer
Local History Room, Fullerton Public Library, and the author

CHAPTER X

Rejuvenation

1970–1990

By the time the 1970s rolled around, a pattern had been pretty well set for Fullerton's future. There were continuing indicators of growth, the population increasing and new construction soaring to all-time highs, and the future was bright—three more institutions of higher learning were on the horizon and a new main library was immediately ahead—but there were also signs that revitalization was needed in some areas. That meant redevelopment planning was in order. Thus, while Fullerton's 1970s and 1980s were times of continued growth, they were also periods of rejuvenation.

A lead role in both areas—handling the continued demands of growth and preparing for revitalization through redevelopment—fell, for a large part, upon government. Local officials made plans to meet resident's needs, including the construction of new civic facilities.

A New Main Library

Capital civic improvements were focused on what has been a community institution since 1888—the library. The 1960s witnessed construction of the Hunt Branch Library followed by firm recommendations for construction of a new main library. By the end of 1969 the groundwork had been laid for turning to the people, and the city did, in April 1970, when voters approved formation of a joint powers authority to finance a new library. Building authority bonds in the amount of $1.3 million were issued in February 1972, a construction contract was awarded in March, and groundbreaking ceremonies were held on April 5, 1972. Construction of the split-level, 50,000-square-foot facility at 353 West Commonwealth Avenue took fourteen months, with the $1.36 million facility ($1,120,000 for the building, $30,000 for landscaping and parking lot and $210,000 for fixtures and furniture) opening to the public on June 25, 1973, one day after dedication ceremonies.

The custom-designed library opened with forty-five thousand square feet of its space developed and with 150,000 volumes on its shelves. It has public meeting rooms, expanded reference services, interlibrary loaning, copy machines, services for the blind and many other special features, including the

Launer Local History Room where the great majority of research for this book was done. Fullerton's free public library system has grown in size and usage despite a multitude of fiscal challenges, and in 1990–1991 the library circulated 1,285,027 books, its reference department responded to 116,045 inquiries, its facilities housed more than 260,000 volumes, 2,980 video cassetts, 602 films, 8,856 recordings, 2,798 compact disks, and it subscribed to nearly 500 magazines and 16 newspapers.

Fullerton's reputation as an academic center—an institution of local concern since 1888 when the Fullerton School District was formed—continued to expand in the 1970s with the addition of three post-secondary institutions. Joining Fullerton College and California State University, Fullerton, were:

It is most fun in a pictorial history to write about an old building which modern readers may still go visit. This building at the northwest corner of Harbor (then Spadra) and Amerige avenues was built in 1901 to house the local order of Masons—Fullerton's first Masonic Lodge with lodge offices upstairs and commercial businesses on the lower floor. The structure—more recently identified principally as the Book Harbor Building—was devastated by fire, but was completely and faithfully restored and reopened in 1992. Photo by the author

Southern California College of Optometry

The Southern California College of Optometry—the third oldest of twelve advanced school of optometry in the United States when it came to Fullerton in 1973—opened its doors here after having six addresses in Los Angeles. Here it has remained, at 2001 Associated Road (northwest corner of Association Road and Yorba Linda), north of CSUF in East Fullerton's "academic square," which now houses four colleges. The school, known as Los Angeles College of Optometry when it moved here, was founded in 1904 by M. B. Ketchum, M.D. and ownership remained in the Ketchum family until 1928. The Department of Physics-Optics at USC had charge of operations (with the facility was located on the USC campus) until 1933, when ownership was taken over by an independent, nonprofit group under direction of a Board of Trustees.

After nearly twenty years in their quarters upstairs at 201 North Spadra (Harbor), it was clear that Fullerton's Masonic Order needed enlarged quarters. The result was this edifice at the northwest corner of Spadra and Chapman avenues which was dedicated in "impressive ceremonies" on the evening of December 8, 1920. The building remains today with plans for renovation pending. Hundreds of area visitors were drawn to the open house on the day of dedication, which nearly one thousand Masons, their spouses and guests attended. Charles C. Chapman gave the address of welcome and new officers—Curtis W. Reeve, master; Elija A. Rhynalds, senior secretary; James A. Green, chaplain; John R. Gardiner, marshal; Harry G. Meiser, senior deacon; Layton S. Conover, junior deacon; Elbert D. Johnson, senior steward; Angus McAulay, junior steward; Amos E. Griffin, tiler—were sworn in. Perry C. Woodward was retiring master of the local lodge whose Temple Association, headed by William Lee Hale, president, formed the Building Committee. Photo by the author

Pacific Christian College

Pacific Christian College moved from Long Beach to Fullerton in late 1973

after purchasing the College Park Shopping Center and two adjacent residence halls south of California State University. The school—125 employees and 354 students—initiated classes on their new campus in the fall of the year after making what a PCC brochure called an "excellent investment" in purchasing the property. The Shopping Center at the southwest corner of Nutwood and Commonwealth avenues and the dor-

This is the Optometric Center of Fullerton/ Southern California College of Optometry at the northwest corner of Yorba Linda Boulevard and Associated Road. The third oldest of a handful of advanced schools of optometry in the United States, the school relocated in Fullerton from Los Angeles in 1973. Photo by the author

mitories on the west side of Titan Drive were built in 1964–1965 at a cost of $6.8 million, the brochure said, and the land and buildings were then valued at $9 million-plus. Pacific Christian bought it for $2.5 million, with a $100,000 down payment. The college was home to about 500 students for the fall 1992 semester. A recent development on campus involves emergence of the Pacific Auditorium in space originally housing the Titan Theater. The Pacific Auditorium Foundation board of directors signed a long-term $1-per-year lease for the facility, undertook a $2 million renovation, and will operate it independently of the college. The Fullerton Civic Light Opera Company called the auditorium home during its 1992–1993 season while Plummer Auditorium was renovated.

Western State University College of Law

Western State University College of Law of Orange County moved from Anaheim into fresh, new, architecturally honored quarters at 1111 North State College Boulevard early in 1975, bringing to the community one branch of the largest accredited law school in the state. Dedication ceremonies were held January 25–26, 1975, at the facility on the southwest corner of State College Boulevard and Dorothy Lane. Both Maxwell S. Boas, dean, and Burton Reis, executive director, founders of the institution in 1966, were present for the celebration. The college and the city have obviously been a good mix, as enrollment has grown steadily to where the Fullerton campus hosts about half of the three-campus enrollment of 2,430 at this writing. There are 55 full-time faculty and more than 100 judges and lawyers serve as part-time faculty at the school which boasts more than 9,000 graduates.

But even in the midst of such growth and prosperity, the community did not escape tragedy. The largest single episode of violence ever recorded in Fullerton—

Pacific Christian College purchased buildings from College Park Fullerton and moved onto its campus south of California State University in late 1973, transferring faculty and student body (325) from Long Beach. About 500 students were enrolled for the fall semester, 1992. Photo by the author

most certainly California State University, Fullerton's darkest hours—focused the eyes of the world on the community.

Tragedy on Campus

In the Monday morning hours of July 12, 1976, death stalked the rooms and corridors of the basement and first floor of the CSUF library. Edward C. Allaway, a 37-year-old campus custodian apparently distraught over marital problems, went on a shooting rampage. He moved through the corridors and offices of the Instructional Media Center in the basement of the building, then moved to the first-floor level and then outside, scattering bullets from his rifle at apparently random targets. Nine were shot, seven died. Allaway, taken into custody without incident about an hour after the shootings, was later declared not guilty by reason of insanity by the courts and was sentenced to a state hospital.

Those few minutes on a bright, sunshine-filled morning, "left an irreparable scar on the memories of those whose lives were touched by the loss of a loved one and those who survived the nightmare of that July morning," wrote Bob Dulyea in the spring 1978 edition of the campus magazine *InterComm.* Mary Koehler, writing in *Kaleidoscope, 1959–1984,* a history of the school's first twenty-five years, said "most on campus that day will never entirely forget what they saw, heard and felt," and this writer, in a 1984 historical sketch of the *Daily News-Tribune,* called reporting of the event, "Perhaps the most difficult task ever undertaken by the daily staff." Those who died—Paul Herzberg, Bruce Jacobsen, Frank Teplansky, Seth Fessenden, Deborah Paulsen, Donald Karges, Stephen Becker (son of Dr. Ernest Becker, founding dean of students)—are remembered by a grove of seven trees—The Memorial Grove—planted north of the library.

Western State University College of Law is new Fullerton quarters won architectural honors in 1975 and the building at the southwest corner of State College Boulevard and Dorothy Lane remains imposing and impressive. The institution has an enrollment of about 1,200 on its Fullerton campus. Photo by the author

The 1975 killing of seven people on the campus of California State University is recorded as the largest single episode of violence in Fullerton history, but the lives of those lost are memorialized in the peaceful tranquility of Memorial Grove, a grouping of seven stone pines standing sturdily in a quiet area south of the physical education building. Photo by the author

The academic institutions which sprang up around CSUF and the new main library were new items on the Fullerton landscape — indications that the growth cycle was continuing. But, there were also signs of existing or potential blight. Problems cited in the 1950s with creation of the Master Plan were now becoming more apparent, and a program of redevelopment was in order. City officials planned a course of action, got it started and it vigorously continues today.

Redevelopment

Redevelopment steps—though not called that then—were initially taken in the late 1950s–early 1960s via creation of downtown parking districts, but full-blown efforts are traced to the 1969 establishment of the Fullerton Redevelopment Agency (made up of the City Council members). An agency brochure succinctly states the, "long-term purpose of redevelopment is to stabilize and augment the revenue producing capability of an area, eliminate blight or conditions which may lead to blight, vitalize and improve the community overall." Toward that end, the agency initially, "identified three geographic areas of the city as candidates for redevelopment projects." Officially designated after preparation of redevelopment plans and public hearings were: Project Area No. 1 — Orangefair (including the shopping center), designated in December 1973; Project Area No. 2—Central Fullerton, and Project Area No. 3—East Fullerton (including Cal State, Fullerton), both designated in December 1974. A fourth project area, Project Area No. 4, composed of non-contiguous areas throughout the city but focused on auto dealerships—existing and potential—was designated in late 1991 and is under study for possible projects.

With the guidance of Terry Galvin, Fullerton redevelopment manager, we will review some of the projects undertaken, ongoing and planned in each area:

Project Area No. 1—Orangefair: The Redevelopment Agency set out to "create a new retail commercial center for Fullerton," in this area, according to Galvin. The result has been the building of "an area powerful enough to create more sales than the majority of malls in Orange County," Galvin said. The Orangefair Mall has been revamped; the building of MetroCenter at the southwest corner of Harbor and Orangethorpe is part of a upgrade on the forty-five acres which includes Montgomery Ward; and the Fullerton Town Center—with the Price Club, Fullerton's largest single producer of sales tax revenue, as centerpiece—has been created in what was originally called the "37 Acres Projects."

Project Area No. 2—Central Fullerton: An exhaustive study reached the conclusion that, "Downtown Fullerton is still Downtown Fullerton . . . but not necessarily a retail center," Galvin said. Subsequently, a plan was conceived to preserve it as such, with an "emphasis on facilitating more pedestrian traffic by providing shaded areas via arcades on Harbor Blvd., new walkways, more

The Fullerton Transportation Center celebrated its grand opening in July 1983, and improvements continue in the area with restoration and rejuvenation of the Santa Fe/ AMTRAK building. The center also includes the Orange County Transportation District Bus Plaza, a major bus transfer point capable of handling eight buses at one time and whose passenger shelters are seen in this picture. A parking garage has also been constructed as part of the improvements as has a commercial building at the corner of Pomona and Commonwealth avenues. Photo courtesy of Launer Local History Room, Fullerton Public Library

159

This is a view of the ill-fated arcades built at selected locations along Harbor Boulevard in the early 1980s. The concrete arcades, seen here in the 200 block of North Harbor Boulevard, were controversial from the start, the design being a compromise that won less than unanimous approval and the finished product being the subject of some ridicule. Downtown businessmen signed petitions opposing the arcades, resulting in their dismantling in March of 1984. Photo courtesy of Launer Local History Room, Fullerton Public Library

Thousands of runners taking part in the ten kilometer race initiated and sponsored for years by the North Orange County YMCA and Fullerton Daily News-Tribune are off and running from the corner of Berkeley Avenue and Lemon Street in the 1983 edition of the August classic. Photo courtesy of Launer Local History Room, Fullerton Public Library

efficient lighting, landscaping, better signing. . . ." The original downtown plan included both housing and commercial improvements, but when federal block grant funds became available for housing, it was decided to concentrate redevelopment monies on more commercial areas. The Harbor Boulevard plan ran into some opposition regarding arcade design. This, in turn, resulted in compromise and, finally, an end product "which almost no one liked," Galvin said. The arcades were subsequently removed, but renewed interest in downtown created by the redevelopment effort brought building owners forward with plans to upgrade properties. Their efforts were facilitated by creation of a Rehabilitation Loan Program, resulting in renovating of major downtown structures, including the Chapman Building. The landscaped Harbor Boulevard median and multistory Wilshire Avenue parking facility are highly visible signs of redevelopment, and, in addition, downtown banks—First Interstate, Bank of America, Glendale Federal—took on major private redevelopment projects. Another extensive project, the Wilshire Promenade, is a prime example of a successful housing development (apartments at full occupancy within months of opening).

A very important part of Project Area No. 2 was creation of the Fullerton Transportation Center—an element which, Galvin and other city officials believe, is the hub of the city's future. Fullerton's three railroad stations have been preserved on the site—The Pacific Electric Station (Il Ghiotto Restaurant), the Union Pacific Station (Spaghetti Factory), and the Santa Fe Station, home to AMTRAK and the subject of extensive refurbishing plans. Also constructed in the Transportation Center was the Orange County Transit District Plaza, North Orange County center for the public bus network; an office building at the southwest corner of Pomona and Commonwealth, adjacent to the center; and a parking structure at the northeast corner of Pomona and Santa Fe to accommodate commuters and downtown visitors. Transportation Center projects are ongoing specifically with platform work at the AMTRAK station (which will make railroad conductor's step-stools unnecessary), and extensive planning has started on methods of accommodating new transportation modems—fixed guideway systems, increased commuter and regular trains, and special OCTD commuter buses.

Project Area No. 3—East Fullerton: Galvin acknowledges there were problems in the designation of this redevelopment area, primarily because of its relative newness. But, he said, "Redevelopment is not confined to fixing dilapidated buildings. Blight means things that are substandard, and that includes more than just 'old' things. Redevelopment also means heading off potential problems; to prevent future deterioration and blight. In this case, private development had simply outraced public improvements." Work was needed in such public areas as parking, streets and sewers and projects have been initiated in each. Probably most visible, however, are three major efforts—the Marriott Hotel, the CSUF Sports Complex, and Vista Park. Undoubtedly, the reworking of shopping centers at

Chapman and State College; commercial development at Nutwood and the freeway; the Racquetball World and Radisson Suites Hotel developments were influenced to varying degrees by the redevelopment projects, both undertaken and planned.

Project Area No. 4: Most projects for the zones encompassed by this designation are in the planning stages at this writing, but the objective is to retain Fullerton's auto dealerships. "This is important to all of us," Galvin said. "Combined and considered as a single entity, Fullerton's auto dealerships constitute the second largest source of sales tax revenue for the city." Some dealers have already moved to auto park developments in other cities, and plans for this area are being designed to halt that process by providing public improvements, procedural and financial mechanisms, private sector investment, and the cooperation of residents, private organizations, business and public agencies necessary to assure proper development.

We have seen, through the new projects previously described, that the changing face of Fullerton was not confined to redevelopment and neither was it limited to physical construction. In 1977 a major change in government structure was approved with the conversion from a City Council/City Administrator to a City Council/City Manager format, under which the manager was given greater powers. Then, in a totally different measure of change, the 1970s and 1980s delivered an influx of Southeast Asian "refugees" to Fullerton, adding to the community's diverse cultural mix.

A rekindling of spirit across the nation came directly to Fullerton in 1984 when the city played host to the Olympic Games with Cal State being the venue for team handball competition. This flush of pride was exemplified by an event occurring even before the games began, when, on July 26, 1984, thousands turned out to watch the Olympic Flame carried through the streets of the city by a series of runners. The *Daily News-Tribune* said it was "more than an event; it was a happening."

And so, we see, "rejuvenation" is actually a combination of many processes, all of which will be an ongoing part of Fullerton's "history of the future." Redevelopment will play a key role, partly because it is an imbeded governmental entity, but also because of the essential need to update public facilities and correct miscalculations. But adjusting to future economics, absorbing of new cultures and ideas, and adapting to changing times and needs of the community are also very vital to Fullerton's future. Accomplishing these tasks, and more, will prove the true measure of successful "rejuvenation."

El Dorado Ranch, a site steeped in Fullerton history, is now the residence of the president of California State University, Fullerton. Built at the turn of the century by E. K. Benchley, a rancher and banker who was Fullerton's second mayor, the property once encompassed the land bounded by Spadra Road (Harbor Boulevard), Richman Avenue, Chapman Avenue, and Valley View Drive. Benchley's daughter and son-in-law, Beatrice and Harry Gantz, were the next owners. Gantz, an Army captain and pilot, is believed to have given the ranch its name. His second wife was Lois Weber, "America's first woman movie director." She used a former lookout tower on the property as a studio where she wrote screenplays. C. Stanley Chapman, builder of the Fox Fullerton Theater and son of Charles C. Chapman, Fullerton's first mayor, was the third owner. He and his wife, Alice, raised their family at the ranch, which hosted weddings and Shriners' gatherings with more than five hundred people attending. In the early 1950s, Chapman commissioned his nephew, architect Charles Wickett, to produce a New Orleans–style exterior for the home which was originally of Spanish hacienda design. In 1989, the Chapman family donated the property as the CSUF president's residence. Seen in photos taken in 1984 are the front entrance framed by a pepper tree, and a view of the south lawn from the 84-foot long terrace where Josephine Juarez Engel, born on the property in 1914 and a longtime Chapman employee, is standing. Photos courtesy of Launer Local History Room, Fullerton Public Library

Following a master plan adopted in the late 1950s, California State University, Fullerton, is building for the future. This aerial view, taken May 31, 1992, of the south-central portion of the campus provides ample evidence, displaying in the foreground McCarthy Hall (left) and its laboratory annex under construction. McCarthy Hall is the former Letters and Science Building, the first permanent structure on campus. Langsdorf Hall, the business/ administration building named after the university's first president, is at the center of the photo and beyond it can be seen the excavation for a new office/ classroom building. In the far background are the Titan Sports Complex (center), the Fullerton Arboretum, and the Jewell Plummer Cobb Residence Halls (right). Photo by Pat O'Donnell, courtesy of CSUF Public Affairs Office

CHAPTER XI

POSTSCRIPT

The Promise

The foreword to this tome concludes "It's a story that helps us understand who we are. And, more importantly, where we are going." We would hope the preceeding pictures and text have helped to accomplish that objective, having served to clarify the course Fullerton has followed and the one it will take as it marches toward a new century. In this concluding chapter, with the assistance of two veteran and key city officials, we will take a peek at the future and seek also to find out what is required to make "the promise" come true.

William Winter, retiring in 1992 after twenty years of Fullerton public service, including ten years as city manager, wrote the following in a special report for this book:

"The future of Fullerton will, to a large extent, be a reflection of its past. Its growth since its agricultural beginnings has been carefully guided and has resulted in a well planned, developed and maintained city. Its leadership has been sensitive to quality of place and of being. Challenges are met with the best interest of the city in mind."

Winter made it clear Fullerton's past was never far from his mind as he discussed the future:

"A trend of preservation has been nurtured in the downtown as well as in residential neighborhoods, and will most likely be continued as residents become more aware of and sensitive to Fullerton's heritage. . . . The physical configuration/shape of Fullerton has historically encouraged a sense of community. Residential neighborhoods, public facilities, commercial areas and a base for industry of various types is in place. CSUF, Fullerton College, Pacific Christian College, Western State University College of Law and the College of Optometry will provide future involvement in education and culture to the city's residents, as will activities as the Muckenthaler and Museum Centers."

Therein lies the Foundation for the future. Of that, Winter wrote:

California State University, Fullerton students leave the on-campus Jewell Plummer Cobb Residence Halls on their way to classes in this April, 1991 photo. The $7 million residence halls, with housing for nearly four hundred students, opened in 1988, and are actually an apartment complex with attached parking ramp. The residence halls were named in honor of Dr. Jewell Plummer Cobb, retiring CSUF president, in 1990. Photo by Pat O'Donnell courtesy of CSUF Public Affairs Office

"Neighborhoods will recycle as younger families of greater ethnic diversity purchase homes throughout the city. This will cause a renewal and continuation of interest in community service programs, etc. In summary, rapid, unmanageable change or problem development is not anticipated. With continued, concerned leadership Fullerton will remain a wonderful place to live and work.

"Fullerton is currently the regional center of northern Orange County, but will play an even more important role as planned transportation links and improvements become a reality. AMTRAK, Metrorail, freeways, super streets and our airport will bring about changes not now envisioned. The diversity of both the city's housing stock and economic base will continue, blending established areas with new development throughout the city."

This evaluation was shared by Redevelopment Manager Terry Galvin:

"Fullerton will become even more of a transportation hub than it now is, as fixed guideway systems are put in place, the number of commuter trains increases and trains are added to the Los Angeles to San Diego and Riverside to Los Angeles routes. Many don't realize that Fullerton is the junction for rail transportation to Chicago and San Diego—the tracks split here. That is why we have asked for more space of AMTRAK in the station remodeling. They are going to need it."

Plans for the fixed guideway system (such as a monorail) include the Fullerton Transportation Center as a major station. One route has stations scheduled at Orangethorpe/Harbor and at Hunt-Wesson. Another route extends eastward along railroad right of way, then north along State College with stations at the university and at the Brea Mall, Galvin said. "The main link is to the west along the railroad to Norwalk, where connections can be made to the 'Green Line,' which can carry you all the way to LAX."

Galvin, confining his remarks to the redevelopment area, also agreed that housing will be an increasing concern. As an example, he linked future housing in the downtown area with his thoughts about the transportation center.

"The future will see a change in emphasis toward housing, partly because current legal requirements on distribution of funding will force it but also because, in the downtown area, we want to create generators as well as destinations. The transportation center needs both."

Galvin sees the downtown commercial area as offering "something different" than what is available in the malls, which, together with public services offered, will generate traffic into the area. Likewise, mall offerings will draw downtown residents to them, and central area dwellers will be commuting to outside jobs.

And what will it take to get there? Winter cited "fiscal responsibility and affordable priority setting," as prerequisites to past and future success. Galvin talked about changing times and a need to respond to them with new ideas and adjusted, creative financial methods.

In contemplating the future, one might do well to review history. As former City Manager Winter suggested when writing, "The future of Fullerton will, to a large extent, be a reflection of its past," history's lessons can, and do provide guidelines for the future. Cooperation and planning have been hallmarks on Fullerton's successful progression through the 130 years since arrival of it's pioneers and the 100-plus years since a townsite survey stake was driven by the Amerige brothers at Harbor and Commonwealth. More of the same will most certainly help fulfill the promise of a bright future.

City officials taking a look into the future have pictured the community as the regional center of the north county area, becoming even more so as new modes of transportation come into being and Fullerton becomes their hub. The city is preparing for that, and one improvement is centered on the Fullerton Transportation Center where improvements to the AMTRAK station began in 1992. Part of the project involved raising platforms at the train station and the building of new shelters and planters. Photo by the author

PROFILES IN LEADERSHIP

Cities are in large part a reflection of the quality and success of their economic and cultural institutions and the people who manage them.

From the earliest times, Fullerton has been blessed with people and institutions of foresight and tenacity. The detailed stories of some of the best are told in the following pages.

FULLERTON MUSEUM CENTER

The Fullerton Museum Center, located in historic downtown Fullerton, complements the City's cultural center with unique changing exhibitions in the cultural arts, science, and history. The Museum has become a significant point of interest in the downtown area by drawing thousands of people a year to its exhibitions, special events, and programs. The history of the Museum begins over a hundred years ago on the corner of Pomona and Wilshire Avenues at the Gem Pharmacy, which was owned and operated by Mr. and Mrs. William Starbuck. Later, with the help of donations from local residents, the Starbucks began the first Traveling Circulating Library in the back room of their pharmacy.

The interior of the Carnegie Library, circa 1950s.

As the city of Fullerton grew so did the need for educational resources. As a result, a larger reading room was established downtown, on the corner of Harbor Blvd. and Commonwealth Ave. In 1904, the Mayor C. C. Chapman proposed constructing a city library. Mr. Starbuck donated his land for the location of the new library and in 1907 construction was underway. To expand construction, the city purchased the two lots next to the intended library for ten dollars from Walter and Mary Skillman. The development of this acquired land was augmented by a grant from the Works Progress Administration while local architect Harry Vaughn, known for his work in the Spanish Colonial style, was hired to design the library building. On Christmas Eve of 1941 the Carnegie Library was complete.

The structure was built consisting of two wings and two courtyards as well as many decorative touches, such as the elaborate molding around the doorways; gold and turquoise Italian mosaic tiles; cast iron entrances; and the long, handmade tiled roof with the ornate cupola at its apex. The most captivating feature, even to this day, are the many hand painted windows of fired, lead glass.

The Fullerton Museum Association was founded in June 1971 by members of the Youth Center Board of Trustees and other interested citizens after signing a lease with the city for the library, which in 1973 moved to its present location on Amerige and Short Street.

"Muse 9" opened at the site of the former library in April of 1974 with its first permanent collection: an assemblage of bones acquired from the LaBrea Tar Pits. To attract a broader audience "Muse 9" was renamed the Museum Association of North Orange County and on February 21, 1985, the Museum took on its present name of the Fullerton Museum Center.

Fullerton Museum also underwent renovations in 1985 and has since become an estimable cultural resource for the city of Fullerton and many surrounding cities. Guided by a mission to develop and present the best in multidisciplinary exhibitions and educational programs, the Museum has curated popular exhibits and has hosted traveling shows including everything from political cartoons to the Titanic disaster to electric guitars.

The Museum also has an active educational program and provides tours, speakers, children's activities, presentations for schools, and other special programs. With a dedicated group of volunteer docents, the Museum provides tours for thousands of people annually, the majority of which are school children.

The Fullerton Museum Center offers a rewarding and enjoyable experience for people of all ages. A visit to the Museum provides the experience of quality exhibitions and activities which stimulate dialogue, promote critical and creative thinking, and act as a vehicle to learn about one's self and our world.

Harbor Boulevard, Downtown Fullerton, circa 1950s.

Fullerton Museum Center, 1989.

Hunt-Wesson, Inc. is one of the largest and most successful food companies in the nation with hundreds of widely-recognized, top selling brand name products distributed across the country and world wide—Hunt's tomato products, Wesson Oils, Peter Pan Peanut Butter, and Orville Redenbacher's Popping Corn products, to name just a few.

With headquarters located in Fullerton, California and manufacturing and sales facilities in many parts of the United States, Hunt-Wesson, Inc. has grown steadily since its rather modest beginnings.

Incorporated in 1890 as the Hunt Brothers Packing Company in Santa Rosa, California, most of those first goods were delivered by horse-drawn carriage. Brothers Joseph and William Hunt established their company and its products as the finest around. As their quality reputation grew and sales increased, the company relocated to larger headquarters in Hayward, California.

Meanwhile, in the small Orange County community of Fullerton, California, a young entrepreneur named Norton Simon was making a name for himself in the canning business. He started Val Vita Food

Products in 1934 and, within a decade, boosted annual sales from $45,000 to $9,000,000.

In 1943, Hunt Brothers Packing Company was merged with Val Vita, and the new company—Hunt Foods—was located in Fullerton, and headed by Simon.

As the years went by, Simon established a can-making plant, a glass plant, innovative nationwide distribution, advertising and marketing programs, and new products. Through these and other smart business moves, including mergers and acquisitions, Norton Simon catapulted the company to a position of national leadership.

The company, which had become Hunt Foods and Industries in 1956, reached a new milestone in 1960 when the Wesson Oil and Snowdrift Company was merged with Hunt's, becoming Hunt-Wesson Foods.

In 1968, a consolidation of Hunt-Wesson Foods, Canada Dry Corporation, and McCall Corporation, came together to form Norton Simon, Inc., a new billion dollar corporation, located in New York City. Hunt-Wesson headquarters, however, remained in Fullerton.

In the meantime, Hunt-Wesson continued to grow through marketing, expansion of its tomato and oil products, and a series of new products. Acquisitions also played a significant role, perhaps the most notable being the purchase in 1976 of the Orville Redenbacher Gourmet Popping Corn operation. In a few short years, creative marketing and sales made it the number one popcorn in the nation. Sales had passed $1 billion for Hunt-Wesson by 1979.

In July 1983, a series of important changes began when Norton Simon, Inc., was purchased by Chicago-based Esmark, Inc., who in turn, was acquired by ConAgra, Inc., a $20 billion diversified corporation, based in Omaha, Nebraska.

As a result of the many mergers and acquisitions, several important product lines were integrated into the Hunt-Wesson family, including Peter Pan Peanut Butter, Swiss Miss drink mixes and puddings, La Choy Oriental Foods, and Rosarita and Gebhardt Mexican Foods.

Through all the changes, with nearly 8,000 employees world-wide and annual sales close to $2 billion, Hunt-Wesson has maintained its leadership position in the food industry. Its headquarters operations and one of its tomato processing plants remain in Fullerton—home for more than 50 years.

Hunt-Wesson headquarters.

FULLERTON SAVINGS & LOAN

When the Guardian Holding Company of America decided to start a building association in Fullerton, they probably didn't realize what a long-term effect it would have on the community. Today, Fullerton Savings has weathered many storms and continues to provide exceptional products and services to Orange County.

In 1927, Guardian Holding Company contacted seven prominent businessmen to open the doors of the Fullerton Building and Loan at 107 West Commonwealth Avenue.

Soon after the Great Depression hit, placing the building and loan on a rocky path for several years. Guardian Holding Company, like many other financial institutions, went into receivership. To protect its interests, Fullerton's Board of Directors purchased the shares controlled by the holding company and continued to operate the building and loan.

To further ensure the stability of the Association, the primary stockholders surrendered their dividends. And Otto Miller, the Association's director, provided additional money to pay dividends to other shareholders and allow for complete withdrawal of each account. Although the building and loan managed to stay in business, its assets dropped considerably.

In 1941, Merrill Gregory became the secretary of the Association. At the same time, the Fullerton Building and Loan relocated to 133 West Amerige Avenue.

During the war years, interest rates were artificially controlled. People started saving more, but the demand for loans was down. The Association began to grow after gaining membership in the Federal Savings and Loan Insurance Corporation (FSLIC).

Following the war, the demand for housing loans exploded and Fullerton began to expand. By the late 1940s, the Association's assets reached $1.3 million, a far cry from its starting assets of $140,000. The housing market continued to expand throughout the 1950s, and higher interest rates attracted new deposits.

In 1962, Fullerton moved to its present location at 200 West Commonwealth at Malden. Continued growth resulted in the creation of five more branches conveniently located in Yorba Linda, Placentia, Anaheim, Garden Grove, East Fullerton, and West Fullerton.

Our financial strength has steadily increased over the years. At year-end 1992, our assets totaled nearly $316 million. Even through the difficult times, no depositor has ever lost a dime of insured—or uninsured—deposits. We pride ourselves on this commitment to our community.

LOMA VISTA MEMORIAL PARK

The Loma Vista Memorial Park has served the north Orange County area for more than three-quarters of a century. The cemetery was founded in 1914 by Argus Adams and Emanuel Smith. The Adams and the Smith families moved to the Fullerton area at the turn of the century. The 37.5 acres originally were purchased from the Bastanchury family.

Grandson Richard L. Adams is now president of the park. The original entrance of the inter-denominational cemetery was on Rolling Hills Drive in Fullerton. The current entrance at 701 East Bastanchury was constructed in 1966.

Many of the Fullerton Pioneer families are interred at Loma Vista. The McFaddens, Spragues, Key, and Chapman families are a few. Author C. S. Forester, who wrote *Captain Horatio Hornblower* is one of our most illustrious tenants. Walter and Cordelia Knott of Knott's Berry Farm also reside here.

One of the most exciting holidays for Loma Vista is the Memorial Day celebration which has been a tradition dating back for more than fifty years. In 1939, C. Stanley Chapman, a World War I veteran and the son of Fullerton's first mayor, began the tradition of putting crosses and flags on each of the more than 2900 veterans' graves. Adorning the front of the park as well as along the streets within are 500 large veterans flags which have been donated by the veterans' families. This spectacular scene is known as the avenue of the flags.

Beautiful stain glass windows and imported Italian marble were used in the 1934 construction of the mausoleum. Additional units have been added with the last one being built in 1960. Our newest additions at Loma Vista are the San Juan and San Miguel garden crypts and niches built in 1989 and 1992, respectively. Our Southern California Spanish heritage is reflected in the architecture of the structures. Already 75 percent sold, another addition, San Carlo, is in the process of being constructed. Also on the drawing board are family garden burial sites as well as the opening of our newest lawn, Sunset.

An alternative to the more traditional form of burial is cremation. With the growing popularity of cremation in the United States, especially in California, Loma Vista has provided this service since 1972. Currently, we have performed over 18,000 cremations. Kurt Adams, great grandson of the founder, is director of West Coast Cremations as well as manager of Loma Vista. Kurt also is a former board member of the Orange County Funeral Directors Association.

Years of good solid community relations, honest service, and old fashioned family values has made Loma Vista Memorial Park one of the most respected businesses in Fullerton.

Argus Adams, one of our founders, 1867–1971

Mausoleum started in 1934

Memorial Day

BECKMAN INSTRUMENTS, INC.

Beckman Instruments, Inc., has been head-quartered in Fullerton for more than 40 years.

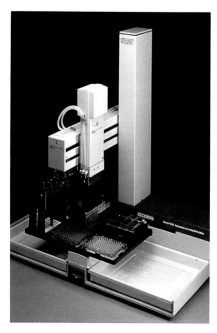

Scientists working on the Human Genome Project are using Beckman's Biomek® 1000 robotic workstation in their study of DNA structure.

Beckman's business is focused on the chemistry of life. The company designs, manufactures, sells, and services a broad range of laboratory instruments and accessories that help advance scientific discovery and speed the diagnosis of disease. Headquartered in Fullerton for more than 40 years, the company produces products for the health care marketplace, and products for life sciences research, product development and quality assurance.

The company dates back to 1935 when a young chemistry professor at the California Institute of Technology used his skill and inventiveness to build a simple pH meter for a scientist friend. This professor, Dr. Arnold O. Beckman, soon left teaching to develop other indispensable tools used by scientists throughout the world to improve the quality of our lives.

In 1940, his new company introduced a second landmark invention: the DU® Spectrophotometer. This critical research tool revolutionized chemical measurement to the point where many scientists divide the history of biochemistry into two distinct periods, pre-DU and post-DU.

Subsequent discoveries led to Beckman's infrared spectrophotometer, the first helical potentiometer, the first commercial oxygen analyzer, the first analytical ultracentrifuge, and a number of instruments invaluable in biological research.

In the field of clinical analysis, Beckman diagnostic systems and chemistries efficiently handle the wide variety of hospital testing needs, providing doctors with critical patient results in seconds. Some of the medical applications include diagnosis of diseases of the heart, kidney, bone marrow, thyroid, and other related ills.

Health care strengths are augmented by Beckman's internationally recognized instrumentation and supplies for biomedical research. The company's bioanalytical products help in the study of living systems and the mechanics of disease, and are applied to virtually every research discipline, such as genetics, immunology, and virology. In addition, the company is also expanding its base in the bioindustrial field, addressing the needs of scientists in pharmaceutical, agricultural, food and beverage, and biotechnology laboratories.

With 6,200 employees in 35 facilities worldwide, Beckman works in partnership with the scientific community to provide the leading-edge technology required in today's laboratory.

It is Dr. Beckman's belief, as well as the philosophy of the company he founded, that there is truly "no satisfactory substitute for excellence."

UNOCAL

A Bible-toting easterner with an uncanny eye for oil prospects and a readiness to take a risk was the driving force behind the enterprise that became Unocal.

When Lyman Stewart came to Southern California in 1883, he was already well acquainted with the boom-and-bust ways of the fledgling oil industry. He had learned them as a sometimes successful oil prospector in his home state of Pennsylvania.

Riding on horseback through the brushy canyons of Ventura County, Stewart hunted for oil in the hills of north Santa Paula. In 1888 he and his partner, Wallace Hardison, brought in California's first gusher. Two years later, with another partner, they founded Unocal, producing oil and gas from the Newhall to the Santa Paula area.

The young company began producing oil from the Brea-Olinda area in Orange County at the turn of the century. Success there led to the acquisition of property in Fullerton in 1907 in what became the East Coyote field, with Unocal's first production in the field coming in 1913. Both these early fields are still producing today.

COYOTE HILLS EAST SPECIFIC PLAN

This is an artist's rendering of the "new" look that Unocal is giving an "old" oilfield in Fullerton. Unocal plans to continue operations in the field for many years.

During the Great Depression, the bottom fell out of gasoline sales and turned the crude market upside down. Although exploration and drilling continued, the company endured five years of production cutbacks during the 1930s.

On December 7, 1941 the Japanese attacked Pearl Harbor, hurling the United States into World War II. Suddenly, the war effort was all that mattered. The military's thirst for oil was insatiable. By the end of 1942 Unocal was producing oil from 1,566 wells, mostly in California.

After the war ended Unocal mounted intensive exploration efforts in Louisiana, Texas, and California with great success. In the 1950s the hunt took the company to Alaska, Argentina, and Australia. The 1960s were enormously productive. Unocal made a major strike in its own back yard, the Las Cienegas field directly under the streets of Los Angeles. The 1970s saw Unocal move successfully into Indonesia, Thailand, Great Britain, and the Netherlands.

The company weathered the storms of a hostile take-over attempt and drastic drops in the price of natural gas and crude oil during the 1980s by restructuring into the smaller, more focused firm it is today.

Over the years Unocal has strengthened its presence considerably in Orange County. Today the company operates production platforms off Huntington Beach and Seal Beach, and a research center in Brea and another field in Placentia in addition to its two early fields.

As well as the above mentioned fields, the company also develops for commercial and residential use land no longer required for petroleum production. The current activity in the East Coyote Field is an excellent example of the company's ability to not only turn an "oil-patch" into a golf course and residential area, but to do it without destroying the habitat of animal neighbors. In this case, the company is actually going to increase the precious nesting foliage of the gnat catcher, a bird on the endangered species list.

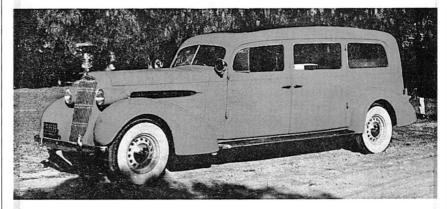

Owned and operated by Angus McAulay from 1911 to 1941.

Owned and operated by A. Jay McAulay from 1942 to 1974.

Owned and operated by William H. McAulay from 1974 to the present with two locations, 902 N. Harbor Boulevard in Fullerton since 1911 and 18311 Lemon Drive, Yorba Linda since 1976.

McAulay & Wallace Mortuary
Funeral Directors and Florist

McCOY & MILLS

Customer satisfaction and community involvement are family traditions at McCoy & Mills. Located on Commonwealth Avenue in the heart of Fullerton, the family owned and operated automotive dealership has been part of the city's history for over sixty years.

McCoy & Mills was one of the first automotive dealerships in the county. It was founded by E. R. McCoy and Arlee Mills in 1930 with the purchase of the Fullerton Ford franchise. In 1932, the partners purchased an Anaheim franchise and named it McCoy Ford. After the death of the original partners the children of Mr. McCoy and Mr. Mills purchased the dealerships and continued to operate both dealerships until 1980 when the families separated their interest.

Over the years there have been numerous changes in the marketplace, but one thing that has remained constant is McCoy & Mills' commitment to customer service. As Jim Miller explains, "Personal attention to the customer is the essence of our business." McCoy & Mills Ford is a two-time recipient of the Ford Motor Company's President's Award for Quality. The award is one of the highest honors in the industry and is presented "in recognition of progressive management, sound merchandising practices, high quality standards, and continuing interest in rendering superior service to Ford owners."

As one of the few remaining family owned businesses in the local area, McCoy & Mills Ford is proud of its reputation as a landmark in the Fullerton community. The dealership is looking forward to continuing service to the community for the next sixty years.

FULLERTON METRO CENTER

We, the merchants and owners of Fullerton Metro Center, salute Fullerton's proud heritage and hope to contribute to its even more promising future.

FULLERTON MOTOR COMPANY

The Fullerton Motor Parts that we know today was actually started in November 1934 by Joe and Velda Johnson located at 127 West Commonwealth, Fullerton, California.

In 1934 there were only two other parts stores in all of north Orange County, so the small store at 127 West Commonwealth served automotive parts needs in Buena Park, La Habra, Brea, Placentia, Yorba Linda, and Fullerton. By 1941, the stock required to serve these communities called for more space and the store was moved to larger quarters—next door at 131 West Commonwealth. In 1950, as automotive needs required more and more room, the store and machine shop were again moved, this time to its present location at 140 West Commonwealth.

Over the years, many honors have come to Fullerton Motor Parts from civic and business organizations. Active in school, fraternal, and business associations, president Joe Johnson has been president and a 45-year member of Kiwanis, International; president of the Fullerton School Board; one of the founders and past president of the Southern California Jobbers; president of the Pacific Automotive Show in 1962; past president of the California Automotive Wholesalers Association; and a director of the Automotive Service Industry Association.

THE FULLERTON REDEVELOPMENT AGENCY

"Preserving the past . . . Preparing for the Future."
Since 1973, the Fullerton Redevelopment Agency has been working to preserve the best of Fullerton's past while taking steps to insure a healthy future for the city. Fullerton's four Redevelopment Project Areas have been created to address specific community needs, and have each achieved significant improvements. Accomplishments in each area include:

Project Area 1
Metro Center
Fullerton Town Center
Orangefair Mall
Fairway Toyota
Allen Hotel
Seismic & Rehabilitation Loans

Project Area 2
Transportation Center
Preservation of 3 historic depots
Chapman Building
Downtown beautification
Fullerton Museum Center
Public parking facilities

Project Area 3
Vista Park
Summit House Restaurant
Marriott Hotel
CSUF Sports Complex

The historic Bank of Italy building in Downtown Fullerton.

Project Area 4
Assistance to automobile dealerships to assure a secure retail sales tax base

FULLERTON INTERNAL MEDICINE CENTER

Fullerton Internal Medicine Center (FIMC) has long been at the forefront of innovation and progress. When the Center was formed, more than thirty years ago, the concept of doctors practicing in a group setting was an exception to the well-established rule of individual practice.

FIMC's continuing basic philosophy of "teamwork and technology" was formed under the assumption that a group of physicians provide a greater base of knowledge and a wider range of skills. Over the years, this philosophy has enabled the Center to keep pace with rapid progression of technical aids in diagnosis and treatment and the delivery of comprehensive internal care.

The Center was formed in 1962 when Dr. L. E. Chapin merged his internal medicine practice with that of Dr. Donald Mahony. During the next thirty years, FIMC has continued to grow. Today, the Center has twenty-one Board Certified Internists and two Board Certified Dermatologists, with most Board Certified or eligible in a sub-specialty, and a support staff of 180. The Center is run as a partnership, with all the physicians owning part interest in the practice. They have occupied their main location at 433 West Bastanchury Road, a 36,400 square foot building, since 1973. In addition, they now also occupy the proximate building at 455 West Bastanchury Road. To further serve the growing Placentia/Yorba Linda population, a satellite office is located at 17491 East Bastanchury Road, Yorba Linda.

Fullerton Internal Medicine Center is unique among large centers because all services are concentrated in the field of internal medicine. The twenty-three physicians comprise the group and represent a wide range of sub-specialties, including endocrinology, oncology/hematology, cardiology, pulmonology, dermatology, gastroenterology, rheumatology, gerontology, and general internal medicine.

As an internal medicine group, FIMC sees its strength in diagnosis and the ability to evaluate the condition of every system in the body. Another advantage for the patient is the fact that, in addition to diagnosing a problem, the internist can provide treatment and/or therapy, most often on site.

To aid in the total care of the patient, FIMC has a full range of the most modern diagnostic and treatment facilities. These include a fully equipped clinical laboratory, radiology facilities, (including x-ray and nuclear medicine, fluoroscopy, mammography, ultrasound), and a cardiac laboratory for performing heart studies, (including echocardiograph, holter monitor, stress testing, and a Specht camera for nuclear imaging of organs). Tests performed in the cardiac laboratory are used to treat current heart problems and screen for future heart disease.

Additional facilities include a pulmonary laboratory, physical therapy, biofeedback for stress or pain reduction, and bone densitometry for osteoporosis testing. The services of a full time nutritionist, who also teaches our weight loss program, is available. Stress management services are offered through marriage and family counselors and psychologists. Smoking cessation programs are also offered with the availability of hypnosis, if needed. Dermatology offers the special skill of Mohs surgical techniques for cancer diagnosis as well as the new technology of liposuction.

Dermatology laser surgery is available. New programs include our expanded chemotherapy program and our diabetic education program provided by certified diabetic nurses and dietitian educators.

The Company Employee Health program is geared to providing physical examinations and health monitoring for employees. The program is custom designed to the company's needs.

The Company Health Program and other preventative health and health monitoring and therapeutic services represent FIMC's interest, not only in treating the patient who is sick, but in helping the patient stay well. Perhaps its concern for overall patient health is one reason why 90,000 patients visited the Center last year.

In looking to the future, Fullerton Internal Medicine Center foresees continued growth and progress. The advantages of experienced physicians working together, coupled with a full range of medical services, continue to provide the foundation for successfully meeting the healthcare needs of today and the future.

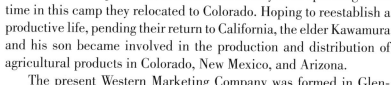

WESTERN MARKETING COMPANY

Western Marketing Company owes its existence to an unusual set of circumstances. As a result of World War II and the evacuation of Japanese Americans from California, Arthur Shinji Kawamura, his wife Kiye, and his son Genji Gene Kawamura found themselves in an internment camp in Gila, Arizona. Eventually after spending some time in this camp they relocated to Colorado. Hoping to reestablish a productive life, pending their return to California, the elder Kawamura and his son became involved in the production and distribution of agricultural products in Colorado, New Mexico, and Arizona.

The present Western Marketing Company was formed in Glendale, Arizona in 1946. Although the firm had expanded and now handles a variety of produce such as lettuce, melons, and cabbage, the decision was made to specialize in the production and marketing of celery. A direct result of this decision was the need to have access to different agricultural regions in order to extend the growing season of celery over a longer period of time. A determination was made to consolidate all operations and branches and move to Orange County in 1953. In moving to Orange County, Western Marketing was exposed and introduced to the then fledgling strawberry shipping industry. This introduction resulted in the eventual expansion of Western Marketing to handle and market strawberries.

Today the third generation of the family, A. G. and Matthew Kawamura, continues to grow and market celery, strawberries, green beans, sweet corn, and other produce throughout the United States, Canada, Europe, and parts of the Pacific Rim. The firm has always stressed quality and service and will continue to do so as it enters its fourth decade in the county.

The future of Western Marketing Company in Orange County will eventually be determined by the continued availability of suitable farmland and water and agriculture in an urban setting continues to be a challenge. As agriculture learns to evolve and adapt so must the consumer it hopes to feed and clothe. Western Marketing has learned to produce and provide fresh produce in an urban environment and plans to continue well into the next century.

Index

181

Bob Ziebell has spent more than 30 years as a journalist in the midwestern and western United States, including a 25-year association with the *Daily News Tribune* in Fullerton, where he was managing editor the last ten years of the daily's existence. Since 1985 he has been engaged in consulting on, and preparation of, business communications and in special writing assignments, most recently as researcher and writer for a newspaper's 75th anniversary publication.

The author has a degree in history from Winona State University in Minnesota. He has been a resident of Fullerton since 1959, where he continues to enjoy life, work, and sharing experiences with his wife, children, grandchildren and friends.

ORANGE
GROVE

W F BOTSFORD